Early Childhood

CONCORDIA COLLEGE LIBRARY
BRONXVILLE, NY 10708

Teachers Guide

CONCORDIA PUBLISHING HOUSE • SAINT LOUIS

Contents

1. Six Great Days (Creation)
2. After the Fall
3. Jacob's Lie
4. Jacob's Ladder
5. Crossing the Red Sea
6. Traveling in the Desert
7. God's Battle Plan for Gideon
8. David, the Singing Shepherd
9. King David and Mephibosheth
10. Elijah's Ups and Downs
11. Naaman, Listen to God's Messenger
12. Jonah, Tell God's Message
13. Three Men Stay Standing
14. Angels and Shepherds Praise
15. Simeon and Anna Meet Baby Jesus
16. Jesus Welcomes Children
17. Jesus Heals Ten Sick Men
18. Jesus Forgives Zacchaeus
19. Two Men Pray
20. The Good Samaritan
21. Jairus's Daughter
22. The Lord's Supper
23. Jesus on Trial
24. Jesus on the Cross
25. Jesus Greets Mary Magdalene at Easter
26. Thomas Sees the Risen Savior
27. Philip and the Man from Africa
28. Rhoda and Friends Pray for Peter
29. God Makes Saul a "New Creation"
30. Paul and Silas Sing for Joy in Jail

Copyright © 2005 Concordia Publishing House
3558 S. Jefferson Ave., St. Louis, MO 63118-3968
1-800-325-3040 • www.cph.org

All rights reserved. Unless specifically noted, no part of this publication may be reproduced, stored in a retrieval system, or transmitted, in any form or by any means, electronic, mechanical, photocopying, recording, or otherwise, without the prior written permission of Concordia Publishing House.

Edited by Carolyn S. Bergt

Scripture quotations are taken from the HOLY BIBLE, NEW INTERNATIONAL VERSION®. NIV®. Copyright © 1973, 1978, 1984 by International Bible Society. Used by permission of Zondervan Publishing House. All rights reserved.

This publication may be available in braille, in large print, or on cassette tape for the visually impaired. Please allow 8 to 12 weeks for delivery. Write to the Library for the Blind, 7550 Watson Rd., St. Louis, MO 63119-4409; call toll-free 1-888-215-2455; or visit the Web site: www.blindmission.org.

Manufactured in the United States of America

Introduction

LITTLE LAMBS TOO

Little Lambs Too is the second part of the Little Lambs Early Childhood curriculum. The title, adding the word *too* instead of *two*, reminds us that little children are an important part of God's kingdom too! This curriculum will follow a style similar to the original Little Lambs, but with a different set of Bible stories (except for essentials like Creation, Christmas, and Easter, which, however, will use a different approach).

As you look at the children in your class, you may think of them as "little lambs." That may also be how they like to picture themselves, with Jesus as the Good Shepherd. Children relate well to this concept; it is not abstract to them. They readily understand their dependency, their vulnerability, the need for someone to take care of them, the need for someone to guide them. Jesus, the Good Shepherd, gives them comfort, safety, and confidence to step out on their own, knowing He is watching over them. He even willingly gave His life to save them, offering them the peace of forgiveness and promised joy in heaven.

This curriculum is active and creative for active and creative kids. It provides opportunities for children to grow in faith in Jesus, to pray, and to play together, relating to Christian adults and becoming part of a Christian community.

The curriculum is meant to be flexible and can be used in a variety of settings. It can be part of your midweek program: while children in grades 4–6 go to Jesus Company (CPH) and children in grades 1–3 go to CrossTown (CPH), the younger children can head off to Little Lambs. This may be part of an evening program, in which parents go to Bible studies, church organizations, and so forth. Or it can be part of an after-school or extended day care or mothers-day-out program. Use it to fit the needs of your children and your church in the area of children's ministry.

This Teachers Guide has an easel back so that each week you can set up the poster picture of the Bible story for the children to see. Leave the picture up throughout the whole session as a constant reminder of your theme for the day. Plus, the other side of the easel will show your lesson plan, readily accessible for a quick glance.

The lesson plan has suggested ideas. But do not feel limited to these ideas. Adjust the order of the activities, eliminate some if you have a shorter schedule, or add routines to fit the needs of your children and your situation. Do keep in mind, though, that the order of activities tends to provide a balance that little children need, going back and forth between lively and quiet activities.

The very fact that this curriculum is for "early childhood" suggests that you may have a wide range of ages in your group. Adjust the activities according to the ability levels of individual children. This is not a one-size-fits-all curriculum. You must make the adjustments necessary, simplifying when needed. Note that the inside cover has a list of teaching hints. You may want to read and implement one of these each week to continually enhance your teaching skills.

A word of caution: Security is very important in this day and age. Insist on a check-in and check-out system for the children. Have parents sign in their children each week rather than just drop them off at the door. Also, do not dismiss children until the parents come in and sign out their child. (If another adult will be picking up the child, the parent must state so in writing when checking the child in.) Parents will recognize that you have the protection and care of their children in your heart and in your procedures.

GATHERING

Your session begins before the "official" beginning time, as soon as the first child enters the room. Have activities ready for the children to explore so that they recognize that this is a place meant just for them. Each week set out familiar items such as puzzles, play dough, blocks, and toys. (The familiar is welcoming and comforting.) As teacher, you will not be directing the activities at this time because children will be making individual choices, but you should be involved in supervision and participation. Use this presession time to talk with individual children and build relationships with them. This is also a good time for simple faith-sharing, one of your most important roles.

In addition to the regular activities you provide for this presession time, add one unique activity of special interest. The Teachers Guide will suggest an activity that relates to or directs the children to the message for the day. *Teaching hint:* As you use this guide, use a yellow highlighter to mark the things you need to prepare in advance.

OPENING

Set up a simple altar in an area of the room set aside as your worship center. The altar may just have a cross on it, or it may be more detailed. But set this area aside as a special place where you gather quietly. Don't have the children seated at tables or desks in this area. In fact, it would be best to be seated with them in a circle on the floor so that you are at the height of the children. Gather the group close to encourage sharing rather than observing.

Begin with simple worship, setting a tone of respect and love for the Lord. Make the sign of the cross on yourself (head, chest, shoulder to shoulder) as you say, **In the name of the Father, Son, and Holy Spirit.** Place your hand on each child's head or shoulder as you move among the children, saying a blessing to each one such as, **God will bless you, God hears your prayers**, or **Jesus loves you.** Feel free to sing a song or say a prayer at this time.

The Opening provides a time of transition as you move into the lesson for the day. Suggestions are given to introduce it with a point of interest to direct the children's attention to the Bible story.

LEARNING

This guide gives suggestions for telling the Bible story in very active and visual ways. Involve the children as much as possible. Refer often to the picture on the Bible story poster in this guide. Another good resource is the *Little Lambs Child and Family Reproducibles*. The Family Page (to be duplicated and sent home each week) can be used as your guide in telling the Bible story. The Reproducible Book also has the children's pages, which are black and white copies of your teaching posters, except that each week there is something that the children will need to add. If time allows, children can color other parts of the picture, or they may take it home to finish it there. Never expect them to color the entire picture.

MOVING

Children need to move. If you don't provide active times, they will be active anyway. Several suggestions are given in the guide; you may want to use the ideas at two different times to break up the schedule. Children of this age are not usually competitive and do not play many organized games. So you will find many of the activities simply involve imaginative ways to get up and move. Repeat activities anytime the children seem restless. You will also find that this is a good time for developing Christian character and putting it into action.

REVIEWING

This section of the guide retells the Bible story with a different technique. Repetition is so important for children of this age; they won't necessarily understand something the first time you say it. So this reinforcement is significant. Plus, little kids love repetition. They like hearing the same story or singing the same song over and over again. The reviewing activities often involve the children in chants or actions.

LIVING

This is the life-application section that relates the Bible story to what is happening in the children's lives. It is at this point, for a change of pace, that it is suggested that you use a lamb puppet. (Lamb puppets and stuffed animals are available at many toy stores, or you can make your own hand puppet from a white sock.) The name "Lucas" is suggested here, but you can use the name of your choice. A puppet script has purposely not been provided because it is best if you consider the recommended concept and then develop it on your own, using the puppet to relate personally to the children. *Note:* It is amazing how the teacher seems to disappear as soon as a puppet is brought out. You don't have to be a ventriloquist. Watch the children's eyes—they are all glued to the puppet. Always have the puppet talk to the children (very rarely to you). Have the puppet move with exaggerated motions to indicate his feelings. Always close with Lucas saying, **Good-bye. God bless you. See you next week.**

SNACKING

Children expend a lot of energy. They need a snack so that they will not feel restless or lethargic. This can be a relationship-building time, and it can be a time to give thanks to God. Finger foods are good for children of this age (have wet wipes handy). Suggestions for fun foods are given, but vegetable and fruit slices are always good. Involve parents in bringing snacks. Or see if several volunteers in your church can take over this part of the program. *Caution:* Be aware of any food allergies that children may have. Also, with young children, avoid chunky foods that children could choke on. And have the children practice good hygiene. (Group settings are always prone to spreading germs.)

This is an important part of your regular schedule, but it is necessary that you choose when it best fits your situation. For example, if children come to Little Lambs after a day of preschool, you may want to start with a snack. If Little Lambs is shortly after dinner time, you may want to delay snack time. For your convenience, all snack suggestions are listed together in the Appendix on the last page of this guide.

SINGING

Song suggestions will be made from *Lift Little Voices*, a printed book with lyrics and music, available from Concordia Publishing House, order no. 12-3331. A CD, order no. 22-2897, is also available that has recordings of 18 of the songs. Always teach songs on the basis of the children's abilities. Do not feel compelled to use all of the suggestions. Occasionally, the children may want to just listen to a new song, rather than learn it. Also do not feel limited to the choices recommended here. Be sure to review songs learned in other sessions. Children love singing familiar songs. Occasionally, optional suggestions will be listed from *Little Ones Sing Praise* and *Songs Kids Love to Sing*, also available from CPH.

Have the first stanza of "I Am Jesus' Little Lamb" be your theme song. (This is not on the CD, but can be found in other music collections for children.) Remember to use any song you learn during your singing time again in your closing worship.

CREATING

Usually two arts and crafts ideas are suggested in this section. You may choose to use just one, or both, or something else entirely. Use what works for your situation. This is an important time for children because what they create is a significant means of communication. It is their "work" and can also be used as their "witness tool" as they explain what they made to their families. *Note:* If you use paint or other messy materials, always have newspapers to protect tabletops, a plastic tablecloth or tarp to protect the floor, large paint shirts or aprons to protect children's clothing, and wet wipes for quick cleanup.

CLOSING

Have your closing at your worship center and use this as a time to wrap up and pull together what has been learned. Then joyfully praise and thank God. Always close with a Bible verse. Read it with your Bible open so the children know the words come from God's Word. Help them develop an appreciation and respect for God's Word. Explain the words and their connection to today's message. Always say the words again and have the children echo them. Then end with a short benediction. Use the same words each week so they become familiar and comforting. Choose words such as, **God bless you and keep you.**

1 Six Great Days (Creation) *Genesis 1*

Theme: God is good.

GATHERING

Set out stuffed animals the children can play with. This will provide a comfortable beginning to what may be a new environment. As the children play, ask them what a real dog (or other animal) can do that a toy dog (or other animal) cannot do. Say, **Today we will learn about the six great days when God made real, live animals and other things on this earth. God is oh so good!**

OPENING

Gather the children around you and say, **I am going to make something—a bird feeder! God made the birds that fly in the air and sing in the treetops.** Loop a piece of yarn through the hole of a bagel and tie it at the top to make a hanger. Spread peanut butter on both sides of the bagel. *Caution: Some children are extremely allergic to peanuts. Find out in advance about any allergies or special conditions of children in your group and make adjustments to activities throughout this series accordingly.* Next, roll the bagel in birdseed. **God made the seeds that grow in the ground. Birds like to eat these seeds.** Hang the bird feeder on a branch outside a window where children can observe birds eating. Say, **I needed many things to make this bird feeder. God didn't need anything at all when He made the world. God just said, "Let it be," and there it was. God is oh so good.**

LEARNING

Display the Teacher Guide poster page for this lesson, but cover it with a large sheet of paper so that you can gradually reveal one line of illustrations at a time. Look at the blank cover sheet and say, **In the beginning there was nothing, except God. So God said, "Let there be light." And there was light. And God saw it was good.** Reveal the first line of the illustration. **When something is good, we applaud—we clap.** Say the refrain "God is oh so good," as you clap once on each word. Have the children repeat it with you.

Continue in this pattern, telling about each day of creation, revealing a line of the picture, and applauding with the refrain. (God made: Day 2—the sky above and waters below; Day 3—dry ground and plants growing there; Day 4—the sun, moon, and stars; Day 5—animals in the sky above and waters below; Day 6—animals and people that live on the earth.) *Note:* It is not important to teach the number of each day. What is noteworthy is that God created the form of His creation the first 3 days, and then He filled it on the next 3 days. God is orderly and wise.

Distribute the children's page. Point out that the two people are missing in the bottom strip. Have the children draw in the two people on their pages as you explain the special ways God created Adam and Eve (see Genesis 2).

MOVING

Have children hold hands in a circle and walk or skip around the circle singing the following to the tune of "Here We Go round the Mulberry Bush."

**This is the way God made the world,
Made the world, made the world.
This is the way God made the world—
He spoke and made it happen.**

The circle should then stop as the teacher says one of the following phrases and the children imitate the actions. Then the circle moves again, and the song is repeated.

Day 1—God made light. *(Quickly raise arms high.)* **Day 2—God made the sky above and the waters below.** *(Point up and then move your hands in low, wavy motions.)* **Day 3—God made dry ground and plants.** *(Pretend to be a tiny seed and "grow" into a large tree.)* **Day 4—God made the sun, moon, and stars.** *(Grasp hands above your head to form the sun; rest head on hands to "sleep by moonlight"; quickly close and open hands to "twinkle" stars.)* **Day 5—God made birds in the air and fish in the waters.** *(Flap arms like birds; place hands together and wiggle them like a swimming fish.)* **Day 6—God made land animals and people.** *(Hop like a kangaroo; sit down and fold hands like a person.)*

REVIEWING

Review the Bible story using a marker and three large sheets of colored paper (which relate to the colors on the poster picture). After each day, chant these lines together:

**And God said "it is good," my friends.
My [first . . .] day is "just right!"**

First, display a sheet of yellow paper and explain that on the first day God made light. Second, display a light blue sheet of paper; draw a wavy line across the middle to separate sky and waters below. Third, display a green sheet of paper to represent the green grass growing on the dry ground; also draw a tree on this page. For the fourth day, go back to the yellow paper and draw the shape of the sun, moon, and stars on it. For the fifth day, return to the blue paper and draw a bird in the air and a fish in the water. For the sixth day, draw a simple animal and two stick people on the green sheet.

LIVING

Bring out a lamb puppet and introduce him as "Lucas the Lamb." Have Lucas tell the children that he knows the next part of the Bible story—on Day 7, God rested. Have Lucas quickly lie down on his side and start to snore. Shake him and tell him to wake up. Lucas can then comment that God must have been tired now that He was finished making the whole world. Then you can explain, **Actually, God's work is still not finished. Just a few years ago, God made each of you children. He held you tightly in a special place under your mother's heart. Then you were born. God is still busy watching over you and blessing you each day. And God takes care of you in a special way through His Son, Jesus, who died on the cross and arose at Easter to forgive your sins. Each day we will learn more about Jesus and how He loves you and saves you. God is oh so good!**

SINGING

Sing the "Thank You Song" on page 34 of *Lift Little Voices* and on its accompanying CD. The song mentions many of the things God created, for which we are thankful.

CREATING

Take the children on a walk and gather items that God created, or provide a collection of such items, such as leaves, grass, flowers, feathers, small rocks, bark of trees, and so forth. Give each child a large sheet of clear contact paper, sticky side up. Have the children lay the found items on the contact paper. Then the teacher or an aide can cover the collage with a second sheet of contact paper. Have the children press their sheets together to "seal" in the items, and hang them in a window or on a bulletin board.

An alternate or additional project is to have the children make circle books of creation. Give each child six plain paper plates. Give instructions slowly, allowing children time to complete one picture at a time. Decorate the plates as follows to represent the days of creation: #1—divide the plate down the center, coloring one half yellow and one half black; #2—divide the plate across the center, coloring the top light blue and the bottom a darker blue; #3—glue on natural plant items like leaves, grass, and flowers; #4—draw a yellow sun and surround it with star stickers; #5—glue on magazine pictures of birds and fish or provide ready-made stickers; #6—glue on magazine pictures of animals and people. Arrange the plates in the correct order, one on top of the other, and staple together on the left side to make a creation booklet.

CLOSING

Remind the children that God rested on Day 7 of that Creation Week. God was not tired; He used that day to enjoy and admire His creation because, as the Bible tells us, "it was very good" (Genesis 1:31). God also wants us to take time each week to appreciate all that He has made and done for us. Each week we set aside time to go to church to learn about God and to thank and praise Him because **God is oh so good!** Conclude each lesson with Bible words to remember, and if your children are able, practice saying the words together. Today, open your Bible to Genesis 1:1 and say, **The Bible is God's own Word. It tells us, "In the beginning God created the heavens and the earth." We praise God for this because He is oh so good!**

2 After the Fall — *Genesis 3*

Theme: I need God's forgiveness.

GATHERING

Set out tarnished pennies, which the children may count or stack. Point out that rubbing the pennies won't change them; you need something special to get them shining like new. Set out bowls with a mixture of ¼ cup vinegar and 1 tablespoon of salt. Let the children use spoons to place pennies in the solution. After a brief soaking, the pennies can be removed and dried with a soft cloth till they shine like new. Discuss how we are like the pennies. **Though our hands may get dirty and need soap to clean them, there is something deep inside us that soap won't help. That something is sin—the bad things we do and think and say. There is nothing we can do to get rid of those sins. But thank God, Jesus has the answer. Jesus died on the cross to take away our sins. Because of Jesus, our sins are forgiven and we are like new people!**

OPENING

Show the children a glass dish. Then show a clear plastic bag that holds a similar dish that has been broken in many pieces. Explain that you broke the dish and there is no way you can ever fix it. You could try gluing the pieces together, but it would never be the same. **In today's Bible story, we will hear about the first people God created—Adam and Eve. They broke God's rule. They sinned. And sin changed everything. Nothing would ever be the same. There was no way that they could fix what they did wrong. It is a sad story, because we are sinners too. But the happy part of the story is that God loves us and He can do all things. So God had a plan to fix the problem of sin. He sent His Son, Jesus, to this world to take away our sins. Only Jesus could do this for us and make things right with God again.**

LEARNING

When God made Adam and Eve and gave them a beautiful home in the Garden of Eden, God also gave them just one rule to obey—they were not to eat the fruit from the tree in the middle of the garden. But the devil, in the shape of the snake, tempted Adam and Eve to sin. Explain, **A sin is doing what we want to do instead of what God wants us to do. The devil made Adam and Eve think the fruit would be something good, but instead it was bad, very bad. As soon as they ate the forbidden fruit, they felt guilty and afraid. They tried to hide from God. They tried to make excuses and blame someone else.** Show the poster picture in the Teacher Guide and say, **God was sad. He knew that everything was changed because of sin. Now, next to the beautiful flowers He created, there were ugly, choking weeds. His beautiful blue sky would often fill with angry storm clouds. Many of His friendly animals would attack others or have to run away in fear. God's strong and healthy people would sometimes get sick or be injured. And all living things would eventually die.** Identify some of sin's consequences depicted on the poster. Distribute the children's page where they can add the thorns to the bush.

Now explain that this story is not just about Adam and Eve. It is about each one of us, because we are sinful too. **Sin is not just what we do wrong, it is also who we are. We are born that way—people are sinners—it is who we are. So even little babies need the help that only God can give. Only Jesus can take away our sins and make us right with God again.** Point out that God didn't wait to give Adam and Eve a hope and a promise. When He told them they would have problems and troubles because of sin, He also told them He would send a Savior. That Savior is Jesus, who forgives our sins so that someday we can go to heaven, where things will be perfect and wonderful as God always wanted our lives to be. **Because of Jesus, we will live in heaven, where there will be no problems, no pain, and no sin.**

MOVING

Talk about the types of movement mentioned in the Bible story, such as walking, crawling, and hiding. Ask volunteers to demonstrate different ways to walk, crawl, or move. Then have the group try each demonstrated movement.

An additional activity is the game Red Rover. Divide the class into two teams. The players hold hands in a line with teams on opposite ends of the field. Teams take turns calling one person to try to break through their line. If that person breaks through, he takes a "prisoner" back to his team. If he does not break through the line, he is "captured" by the opposing team. After the game, sit down to rest and say, **When we break God's rules, we sin. Sin has captured the people of this world; we are prisoners of sin. But sin is not a game. And there is only one way to be rescued. Only Jesus can save us from sin. How did He do that?** (He died on the cross to take away our sin.) **Why did He do that?** (He loves us.)

REVIEWING

Always consider using the Bible story text printed on the family page to either tell or review the Bible story. Children need to—and like to—hear a story repeated often. This will also make a good connection between what is said in your class and at home. After reviewing the Bible story, hold up a large copy of a photo of yourself. Emphasize that today's Bible story about Adam and Eve is also about each of us because we are all sinners who need God's help. Say, **Sometimes we do the wrong thing, something we should not do.** Tear the picture down the center. **Sometimes we don't do the right thing, we don't do something we should have done.** Tear the picture across about one third of the way down the page. **When we sin, we make a mess of things and we can't make it right again. There is only one way that our sinfulness can be fixed.** Turn the pieces over and apply a dark-colored tape (such as black electrical tape) to repair the page while also making the shape of a cross. Hold up the repaired page on the cross side and say, **Only Jesus can help us. He died on the cross to take away our sins. He makes us children of God! When God looks at us, He doesn't see sin, He sees the cross of Jesus, and we are forgiven!**

LIVING

Bring out Lucas the Lamb, who is crying. He feels bad because he was mean to his friend Gertrude. Ask the children if they ever felt sad because they did something bad to someone. Talk about praying to Jesus for forgiveness and then telling the person you hurt that you are sorry. Have Lucas happily bounce away, and then shortly bring him back crying again. He explains that he was drawing a pretty picture to give to his grandma, but the wind came up and blew it into a water puddle. Say, **Sometimes bad things happen with no fault of our own; they happen just because we live in a world that is full of troubles and problems. God promises that someday, because of Jesus, He will take all believers to heaven, where there will be no more troubles or problems or sin. We can trust God's promise.**

SINGING

Say, **God loves us and made a beautiful world for us. Sin spoiled things. But God still loves us. He sent Jesus to save the world.** Read John 3:16 and then sing "God So Loved the World" (*Lift Little Voices*, p. 33 and on the CD).

CREATING

In advance, cut out an 8-inch heart shape from white paper, one per child. At the center of the heart, the teacher should apply wide, clear adhesive tape in the shape of a cross.

Prepare the room and the children for painting (for example, cover tables with newspaper, have children wear protective paint shirts, have wet wipes readily available). Place blue paint in a shallow dish. Children are to paint the heart shapes using 3-inch squares cut from a sponge to dab on paint. (Hint: attach a clip clothespin to each square to use as a handle.) After the paint dries, say, **These hearts are no longer white. They remind me of our hearts that are changed by sin. There is only one thing that makes a difference in our hearts and lives and that is Jesus.** Peel off the adhesive tape to reveal the white cross at the center of each heart.

CLOSING

Close by again singing "God So Loved the World" (*LLV*, p. 33). Then open your Bible to 1 John 2:12 and say, **Listen to this Good News we have from God's Word! "Your sins have been forgiven."**

3 Jacob's Lie *Genesis 27:1–41*

Theme: Families need God's help.

GATHERING
Set out people figurines that children may use to show families working together. Say, **Sometimes families are happy. But sometimes people say or do things that are unkind. That's because we are all sinners. We need God's help. With the love and forgiveness we have from Jesus, we can learn to love and forgive each other.**

OPENING
Display a funny mask (not a scary one). Say, **Let's play a game to see if you can guess who is wearing this mask.** Ask all children to close their eyes while you put the mask on a child. Tell them to open their eyes and guess who it is. Continue till everyone has a chance to play. Then say, **Today we'll hear about a young man who tried to trick his father. He wore something that made him look like his brother. It wasn't a game like we played. His trick caused a lot of trouble in their family.**

LEARNING
Display the poster picture for this lesson. Point to each character as you introduce them. **Jacob and Esau were twin brothers. But they did not look alike; they did not talk alike. Esau liked to go hunting outdoors with his bow and arrow. Jacob liked to stay at home and take care of the sheep. Esau had big muscles and he was very hairy, rough, and tough. Jacob was quiet and had very smooth skin.**

Their father, Isaac, was a very old man. He was blind; he could not see. Isaac decided to give God's special blessing to Esau. That was wrong because God said Jacob should have the special blessing. But Isaac decided to disobey God. He told Esau to go hunting and prepare some food, and then Isaac would give the blessing. Isaac's wife, Rebekah, saw what was happening. She wanted Jacob to get the blessing. So she made a plan to trick Isaac. She was sinning too. She put animal skins on Jacob's arms and dressed him in Esau's clothes. Jacob pretended to be his brother. He lied to his father. Jacob sinned too. When Isaac touched Jacob's arms he said, "It is Jacob's voice, but these are Esau's arms." So Isaac ate the food and gave the blessing. He thought he was blessing Esau, but he was really blessing Jacob. When Esau came home from his hunt, he found out what had happened. He was so angry that he wanted to hurt his brother and kill him. Esau sinned too. Distribute the children's pictures. **Draw angry faces on all four people because they all did something wrong. Sin causes trouble and makes people unhappy. But that is not the end of the story.** Take a heart-shaped sponge (cut in advance) and dip it into red paint. Print the heart shape, pressing it onto white paper and say, **God does not like sin, but God still loves His people. So He sent Jesus to save us.** Take a cross-shaped sponge (smaller than the heart) and dip it into brown paint. Print the cross on the red heart and say, **Jesus died on the cross to save sinners.**

MOVING
Play family charades. Have groups of children pantomime a family activity chosen by the teacher. (Suggest routines such as sleeping, brushing teeth, eating an ice-cream cone, opening a door.) Then say, **May God bless our families.**

Another activity begins by having children line up at a starting line. Ask questions about families and indicate the number of steps to be taken if the answer is yes. For example, **If your family has a pet, take 2 steps; if your family likes spaghetti, take 5 steps; if your family likes boat rides, takes 8 steps.** Count off the number of steps to help those who are still learning to count. Ask broad questions, vary the number of steps taken, and make sure that everyone crosses the finish line about the same time.

REVIEWING
Divide into four groups, one group for each character in the Bible story. Tell them that when you say the name of their Bible story person, they may stand and then sit down. Say, "Let me introduce you to *Isaac, Rebekah, Jacob,* and *Esau.*" Continue:

**Jacob, Esau, mom, and dad—
All were sinners; all were bad.**

Describe each sin as you say, "*Isaac* did not want to follow God's will about the blessing. *Rebekah* made a plan to trick her husband. *Jacob* lied to his father. *Esau* was so angry he wanted to kill his brother." Continue:

**Rebekah, Isaac, and the twins—
No one wins when each one sins.**

Say, "*Isaac* was unhappy. *Rebekah* was unhappy. *Jacob* was unhappy. *Esau* was unhappy. This family was in a mess of trouble." Continue:

**Momma, Dad, and both kids too—
What in the world were they going to do?**

Explain that God had the answer to these problems. He loves and forgives us and He calls us to love and forgive each other. But this family wasn't listening to God's message. Say, "*Isaac* and *Rebekah* told their son to hurry away, escape to safety. So *Jacob* left to live with his uncle for many years. And *Esau* stayed angry for many years." This mess would have been changed if only they had listened to God's message to say you are sorry and admit you were wrong. Continue:

**Oh, this family was in a big mess.
Each one sinned and needed to confess.**

Point out that in our own families, when problems come up, God's plan for us is best. He leads us to say these important words that can make such a difference: "I am sorry" and "I forgive you." Hold an open Bible and say, **Listen to God's Word: "Forgive as the Lord forgave you" (Colossians 3:13).**

LIVING
Bring out Lucas the Lamb, who says Rufus and Rita were fighting. **I tried to make peace. I asked Rufus to say "I am sorry" and he said NO! I asked Rita to say "I forgive you" and she said NO!** Explain that peace does not start with Rufus or Rita, it starts with God. God calls us to repent—to say we are sorry and admit we are wrong. God is always ready with His forgiveness that He offers us through Jesus. With the love and forgiveness of God in our hearts, we are led by God to love and forgive others. It all starts with God. Remember: "Forgive as the Lord forgave you."

SINGING
Read about God's forgiving love in 1 John 4:7–11, 16, and 19. Ask children to raise their hands every time they hear the word *love* (or a form of the word). Sing "Love One Another" (*Lift Little Voices,* p. 41 and on the CD).

CREATING
Ask the children to draw pictures of their own families. Then provide heart- and cross-shape sponges and dishes of red and brown paint so the children can add the shapes to each person in their family pictures. Emphasize that God loves each person and that Jesus died on the cross for each person in the family. Pray together for their families.

For an additional activity give each child a sheet of yellow construction paper. (Model each step of the activity, and also provide practice sheets.) Hold the paper "the tall way" (vertically). Have the children fold the paper from side to side. (Down the center.) Now emphasize that they hold onto the folded, creased edge in one hand. With the other hand, take a scissors and cut a "large box" out of the top corner of the paper (opposite the fold). Then cut a "large box" out of the bottom corner. If done correctly, they will have the shape of a cross when they open the page. Ask the children to draw pictures of their family members on the cross shape. **This reminds us that Jesus died on the cross for each person in your family.** Print these words on each cross: *Jesus died to save us.*

CLOSING
Say, **Our Bible story today was a sad story. A happy ending to any of our family problems begins with the love and forgiveness that only God can give. God leads us to share that love and forgiveness with each other.** Hold an open Bible and read these Bible words to remember from 1 John 4:7: **"Love one another, for love comes from God."**

4 Jacob's Ladder

Genesis 27:42–45; 28:10–22

Theme: God watches over us.

GATHERING
Provide star stickers and black paper so children can make a night sky scene. **Today's Bible story takes place at night, under the stars.** *Option:* Add a title to the pictures with white chalk, saying, *God is with me all through the night.*

OPENING
Display pictures of places such as the beach, the mountains, a grocery store, a church. Direct attention to each one and say, **God watches over us there and everywhere we go.**

LEARNING
In advance prepare a "stone pillow" for each child by wrapping a large book with gray paper. Also have a ladder available. Use the Bible reference and the text on the family page as your guide in telling the Bible story. Begin by displaying the poster picture for last session's Bible story. Say, **Jacob had to leave home in a hurry. Why did he have to escape to someplace safe?** (His brother, Esau, was angry and wanted to kill him.) **Why was Esau so angry?** (Jacob had tricked his father into giving him the blessing that Esau wanted.) Continue with today's story. When you talk about Jacob sleeping outside and using a stone for a pillow, display the poster picture for today. Also distribute the "stone pillows" (paper-wrapped books) to each of the children. Tell them they can pretend to be Jacob by lying on the floor and placing their heads on their "stone pillows."

Point out that Jacob probably felt lonely and afraid. Then God did something wonderful to remind Jacob that God loves us, forgives us, and watches over us. Bring out the ladder and talk about Jacob's dream. Use hand motions to indicate the angels going up and down the ladder in the dream. Point to the top of the ladder as you talk about God speaking to Jacob. Read God's actual words from Genesis 29:15.

Point out that Jacob woke up and was very happy because he knew God was there with him, watching over him. As a reminder of this special event, Jacob set up the stone as a memorial. Have the children stack up their "stone pillows" as a memorial—a reminder that God also promises to be with us wherever we go.

MOVING
Play follow the leader. As you lead the children around the premises, stop frequently and ask, **Is God with us here?** Read Psalm 139:9–10 when you stop to rest. Point out that these Bible verses again remind us that God is always with us.

As an additional activity, go to a stairway in your building and have the children go up and down the stairway several times, like the angels who went up and down in Jacob's dream. Then sit together on the stair steps as you talk to the children about God's angels. Emphasize that angels are a special creation God made. Angels are not people. They are invisible, but they can take on the shape of a person, as we see in several Bible stories. Angels are God's helpers and messengers, as at Christmas and Easter. Some stories in the Bible talk about angels appearing with wings or glowing as bright as lightning. God sends angels to watch over us. Read aloud Psalm 91:11.

REVIEWING
Read this poem, having the children imitate your actions.

(Run in place.)
"Run, run, Jacob, run very fast.
Run, run, run till you're safe at last."
(Rest head on hands to "sleep.")
"Now you are tired and all alone.
Go, rest your head upon a stone."
(Pretend to walk up stairs.)
Then in his dream he heard God talk
As up and down God's angels walk.
(Point all around.)
The Lord said, "Never have a fear.
Where'er you go, I will be near."
(Jump joyfully.)
When Jacob woke, he gave a cheer
And said, "I know that God is here!"
(Pretend to move heavy stone.)
He set a stone to mark the place
Where God gave him forgiving grace.
(Cheerfully, walk in place.)
Now Jacob walked off joyfully
For God would guard him faithfully.

LIVING
Bring out Lucas the Lamb, who has one of the star pictures made earlier. Lucas says the picture is scary because he is afraid of the dark. He is especially afraid of the dark because he is afraid God won't be able to see him and watch over him. Explain that God is so powerful that He sees all and knows all. He can do all things. He can watch over us even when it is dark. After all, God created the light and the dark and He has power over them. God watches over us all the time! Read Psalm 139:11–12.

SINGING
Emphasize that nothing can keep God from us—nothing is too high or too far away or too dark or too light. Teach the children the phrase: *Nothing can keep us from the love of God.* Encourage the children to join in singing that phrase as you listen to the song by the same name (*Lift Little Voices*, p. 43 and on the CD). Another song with today's theme is "God Is with Us" (*Lift Little Voices*, p. 38). Also, read Psalm 121.

CREATING
Say, **God sends His angels to watch over us. Listen to God's Word.** Read Hebrews 1:14. **And listen to these words of Jesus that are especially about angels watching over children.** Read Matthew 18:10. As a reminder, have children make angel pictures (reminding them that, except for certain occasions, angels are invisible and cannot be seen). Tell children to place a shoe on a piece of white paper and use a pencil to draw around it. Cut out the shape. Draw eyes, hair, and a smile on the top part of the footprint. (The rest of the footprint is the angel's robe.) Next place one hand on yellow paper, spread the fingers open wide, and trace around this hand. Do this again and cut out both hand shapes. Use a glue stick to attach these hands to the back of the angel to make wings, with the feathers (fingers) of one pointing to the right and the other to the left.

Another project can be used in connection with today's closing. Provide each child with 6–8 long strips of brown paper. Children are to make Jacob's ladder by placing two long strips almost side by side, a couple of inches apart. Then they are to cut up one or two of the other strips into smaller pieces to make the steps of the ladder and glue them in place with a glue stick. (Suggest that the children give their parents the ladder to use as a Bible bookmark after telling their parents about today's lesson.) Have children keep two brown strips for the closing.

CLOSING
Hold up the paper ladders that you made. Say, **In Jacob's dream, angels went up and down the ladder. God was at the top of the ladder. He spoke to Jacob. God promised to bless Jacob and be with him. But the most important promise God made was His promise to save us. This time God Himself came down. Jesus—true God—came down from heaven to save us from sin. He didn't use a ladder. What did He use to save us?** (A cross.) At this point, glue two brown strips together to make a cross. **God loves us so much that He came down from heaven, was born in a manger at Christmas, and died on the cross to take away our sins. He arose to new life on Easter morning, and even though He went back up to heaven, He promises to always be with us. Listen to the words of Jesus from the Bible.** Read the last sentence of Matthew 28:20. Then open your Bible to Genesis 28:15 and read today's words to remember: **God says, "I am with you and will watch over you wherever you go."**

5 Crossing the Red Sea
Exodus 13:17–15:21

Theme: God knows what is best.

GATHERING
Set out partially filled tubs of water with items to test for sinking or floating. As children explore the water play area, set people figurines atop one side of the container. Ask, **How can these people get to the other side?** (Swim, walk around the edge, ride a boat, build a bridge.) **Today we will hear how God helped real people when they were stopped at the edge of an ocean of water.**

OPENING
Display one block and say it stands for Jacob. **We've learned two Bible stories about Jacob. God forgave Jacob's sins and blessed him with a large family. He had 12 sons.** Set out 12 more blocks. **These sons grew up, got married, and had many children.** Add more blocks; continue this pattern. **The family was so big you could hardly count them. The people were called the children of Israel. Today we will hear about the special way God rescued and saved the Israelite people.**

LEARNING
The people of Israel were slaves in the land of Egypt. (Briefly explain slavery.) **They prayed to God for help, and God rescued them. He sent Moses to lead them to a new homeland.** Hold a wooden stick and pretend to be Moses. Lead the children (as the people of Israel) around the room to a place where, in advance, you have placed two three-yard lengths of blue fabric, side by side on the floor. Perpendicular to these, line up a row of chairs. Say, **The people were afraid they would die. In front of them were the deep, deep waters of the Red Sea** (the blue cloths); **there were mountains to the side** (the chairs); **and now, behind them, their enemies were rushing in their chariots to capture them. The people couldn't swim over the deep, deep waters; they didn't have boats; they couldn't climb the tall mountains; and they didn't have time to build a bridge. The people said, "Why did God let this bad thing happen?" They forgot that God always knows what is best and God is all-powerful. God told Moses to raise his walking stick over the water, and an amazing thing happened.** (Raise your stick and then have four volunteers lift the fabric pieces at the corners to form two "walls of water.") **God separated the waters; they stood straight up like walls. God made a dry path where the people could walk to the other side.** Lead the children in between the walls of blue fabric. Once they are on the other side, raise the stick and have the volunteers place the fabric back on the floor. **When the enemies tried to follow, the waters came down on them. The people of Israel thanked God for saving them. They sang songs to praise God. God knew what was best for the people of Israel. God knows what is best for us too. He loves us and cares for us.** Distribute the children's page. Emphasize that the power to save the people did not come from Moses or his walking stick. The power was in God's command and promise!

MOVING
Divide the children into two or more relay teams. At the starting line, each team will have a bucket of water and a ¼ measuring cup. Across the room each team will have a plastic drinking cup. Demonstrate that at the signal, the first person on each team takes a quarter cup of water from the bucket, runs to place the water in the drinking cup, and returns to hand the measuring cup to the next runner in line. Children are to run the course even if they spill their water. The first team to get their cup filled to the brim wins. (*Option:* Repeat the contest using a tablespoon.) Say, **We had problems with just a small amount of water. Think of the great power of God in the Bible story; He had power over the waters of the sea! God is amazing!**

As another activity, have children hold onto the edges of the blue cloth used earlier. Give directions (much like parachute play): wiggle the fabric a little to make little waves; slowly move arms up and down to make big waves; place Ping-Pong balls on the fabric and ripple the cloth slowly and then faster without dropping any balls.

REVIEWING
Review the Bible story with dialogue and song. Recall that the people were afraid they were trapped and would die. **They forgot to trust God.** Using the melody of "Row, Row, Row Your Boat," have the children repeat each line after you. Sing:

Row, row, row your boat! *(children repeat . . .)*
Sorry, I have none.
Build a bridge! That just won't work.
Nothing can be done!

Moses reminded them God always knows best. Read Exodus 14:13–14. Then sing:

Why, why do you fear?
God will do what's best.
Wait a minute; stop and watch.
God will do the rest.

Note that God made the water stand tall with a dry path in between. Sing:

How can water stand
Straight up and so tall?
God can do it; God knows best,
With power over all.

God saved His people; they rejoiced. Read Exodus 15:1–2, 20–21. Then sing:

Praise, praise, praise the Lord.
He has saved the day!
He has won the victory!
Sing and shout hooray!

LIVING
Bring out Lucas the Lamb, who angrily says, **When I asked my Mom if I could eat five ice-cream cones, she said no. If she loves me, why doesn't she give me what I want?** Explain that she said no because she *does* love him and doesn't want him to get a tummy ache. She knows what is best for Lucas. This is even truer about what we ask of God. When we pray, we won't always get what we want because God loves us and will do what is best for us. Sometimes God will say *yes*. Sometimes God's answer is *wait till the time is right*. And sometimes, when it seems that God is saying *no*, He is really saying *He has a better plan*. Read Jeremiah 29:11 and Romans 8:28.

SINGING
Review "Nothing Can Keep Us" (*Lift Little Voices,* p. 43 and on CD), remembering that the waters of the Red Sea couldn't keep God's love away from His people. God's love and forgiveness are always there for us too.

CREATING
Water is an important element in today's Bible story. Have children use paintbrushes and water buckets to "paint" with water on outdoor concrete or blacktop surfaces. The water designs will appear darker than other areas, but will quickly evaporate. A much more important water connection in this story relates to the waters of Baptism. Say, **God worked through the waters of the Red Sea to rescue the people from their enemies. God also works through the waters of Baptism to rescue us today.** (This is a simple introduction. Baptism will be discussed more thoroughly in later lessons.) Describe what we can see in Baptism—the pastor at the baptismal font in church pours water on a person three times in the name of God the Father, Son, and Holy Spirit. **Baptism is not something we do—it is a gift from God. He promises the gift of forgiveness because of Jesus. In Baptism our sins are washed away, not by the water but by the power of God!**

CLOSING
Read today's Bible words to remember from Psalm 31:6: **I trust in the Lord.** Pray together with hands palm to palm rather than folded. After each prayer petition, you and the children may open your hands wide, like the parting of the waters at the Red Sea, and together say the verse from Psalm 31.

Dear God the Father, help me when I am afraid . . .
Dear Jesus, please wash away my sins . . .
Dear Holy Spirit, help me grow in faith . . . Amen.

6 Traveling in the Desert

Exodus 16:1–17:7

Theme: God gives what we need.

GATHERING

Set out dishpans partly filled with clean sand. Laminate pictures of food; hide them in the sand. Children may search through the sand to find the pictures. As they do so ask, **Where do we get the food we eat?** (At home in the kitchen, from the grocery store, at a restaurant, and so on.) **Actually, the food we have is a blessing from God. The Bible says, "Give thanks to the Lord, for He is good" (Psalm 107:1).**

OPENING

Bring a colorful lunch bag filled with nutritious snacks such as fruit, cheese and crackers, and carrot and celery sticks. Ask the children to guess what foods are inside it and then show them (and perhaps share some). Say, **When God's people, the Israelites, were traveling through the desert, they didn't have lunch bags. There were no fast-food restaurants or grocery stores along the way. There was only dry sand and rocks. How do you think they got the food they needed when they were hungry? Let's listen to find out how God gave them just what they needed.**

LEARNING

Refer to last week's Bible story and the marvelous things God did for His people, freeing them from their enemies and rescuing them at the Red Sea. But soon the people forgot about the wonders and goodness of God. Time and again they grumbled and complained, and time and again God was patient. He forgave them and helped them. Using the Bible reference and family page text, emphasize this repeated pattern as the people received bread (manna), meat (quail), and water (from a rock) by God's gracious blessing. Note: When you talk about manna, have the children sit in a circle and close their eyes. Sprinkle frosted flake cereal on a large sheet of mural paper at the center of the circle. Have the children open their eyes. Say, **God blessed the people. When they woke up, they saw food lying all over on the ground. It tasted like wafers of bread or cereal, with a sweet flavor like honey.** Give each child a bowl of the wafers. Point out that God did not want them to be greedy. They were to take only what they needed for that one day. God wanted them to trust He would help them again the next day. God also wants us to trust Him for what we need and to be thankful for all the good gifts He gives to us.

Distribute the reproducible children's picture. Encourage them to draw manna on the ground and in the bowls. Then read this poem, remembering God's abundant blessings.

**See quail from above and
Manna on the ground!
There's water from a rock!
God's love is all around.**

MOVING

Play a hide-and-seek game. Take the laminated food pictures from the presession activity and hide them around the room. Let the children hunt for the pictures.

For an additional activity, children may make play-dough food to place on paper plates. **Your play-dough food looks great. But I would not want to eat it. Thank God that He gives us food that looks good, smells good, and tastes good!**

REVIEWING

Discuss what a desert is like. Then discuss the words *grumble* and *complain*. Point out that the people of Israel often forgot about God's loving care. But God was patient and forgiving. Read this poem, letting the children repeat each line after you.

**We're traveling in the desert.
We grumble and complain.
It's hot and very dirty here.
(Each part of me feels pain.)**

Point out that the people complained about not having bread to eat.

**We're traveling in the desert.
We grumble and complain.
We do not have some bread to eat
For there's no flour or grain.**

God gave them bread (manna). Still the people complained. They wanted meat too.

**We're traveling in the desert.
We grumble and complain.
We'd like some meat with special sauce.
(I'd even eat it plain.)**

So God gave them meat (easy-to-catch quail). And yet the people complained. They didn't have enough water.

**We're traveling in the desert.
We grumble and complain.
There is no water we can drink,
And there's no chance for rain.**

Point out that we are no different than the people long ago. We grumble and complain if we don't get what we want. Pray, **Dear God, please forgive us when we grumble and complain. Thank You for being so patient with us. Help us to trust You to give us what we need. Help us to be thankful for these blessings. Amen.**

LIVING

Bring out Lucas the Lamb, who tells how his shepherd finds food for him to eat and water to drink. Point out that God's Word compares us to sheep, and the Lord God is like a Good Shepherd who gives us what we need. Hear God's Word in Psalm 23. Explain each verse as you read it, giving the children a word picture of ourselves as happy sheep and Jesus as the shepherd who takes care of us, giving us what we need, protecting us from danger, and leading us home to heaven.

SINGING

Sing together the "Thank You Song" (*Lift Little Voices*, p. 34 and on CD). You may even want to add extra stanzas, changing the words to speak of various kinds of food and other blessings we receive from God.

CREATING

Emphasize that God not only gives us what we need, He gives us what we need most—the forgiveness of sins and eternal life we have through Jesus. Make pictures to show how Jesus saved us. (By dying on the cross to take the punishment for our sins.) In advance, mix powdered tempera paint into containers of clean sand. Have children draw a large cross on paper (or let them trace around cross-shaped cardboard patterns you have made in advance). They may cover the cross with white glue and then pour colored sand onto the glue. When the glue is dry, shake off the loose sand into a container. *Option:* Add extra layers of glue to outline the cross, using the same technique but using a different color of sand with each layer.

For an additional project with a message, give a rectangle of sandpaper to each child. Display this three-character message: the letter *I*, a heart shape, and a cross shape. Explain that this says, "I love Jesus." Children are to draw the message on the sandpaper with crayons, using a different color crayon for each letter and shape.

CLOSING

Open a Bible to today's words to remember from Psalm 107:1: **Give thanks to the Lord, for He is good.** Ask children to think of blessings from God. These can be types of food, but God also blesses us with so many other things, such as pets, parents, toys, and so on. Point to each child who volunteers. The child can stand, say what the blessing is, and then everyone can respond with the Bible words.

7 God's Battle Plan for Gideon

Judges 6–7

Theme: God is almighty.

GATHERING
Play tug-of-war. Mark a middle line on the floor with masking tape. Put equal numbers of children on both ends of a rope. Teams pull until someone on the other side is pulled across the line. Step in and join their game, but say, **There are too many people on this team.** Send all but one child to the other team. Pull hard (and be sure you win!). Ask if your team won because the child on the team was the biggest, strongest, or bravest. (No, it's because the teacher was powerful.) Explain, **Today we will see that God's people won a victory, but not because they were the biggest or strongest or bravest. They won because the power of God was on their side.**

OPENING
Turn off the lights in the room. Then make a loud noise, dropping a book or metal bucket on the floor. Say, **Sometimes a crashing noise can be scary.** Turn on the lights and say, **Sometimes a sudden bright light can be scary.** Shout *"hooray"* and say, **Sometimes a loud shout can be scary. This was part of God's plan to get rid of the enemies of His people. God used crashing noises, bright lights in the night, and loud shouts to scare the enemy away. Let's learn more about God's plan.**

LEARNING
Say, **The Midianites were enemies of the Israelite people. The Midianite armies came into the land of Israel and stole their food, captured their animals, and took their money. The people of Israel cried to God for help. God chose a man named Gideon to lead the people of Israel. Did God choose the best soldier or the strongest general in the army? NO! In fact, this is what Gideon said to the Lord: "No way! I'm not a soldier. I'm a farmer." But God said that didn't matter, because God had the power. God would win the victory.**

For the next part of the story, to represent Gideon's army, set out a large number of toy soldiers or clothespin puppets that have "smiley faces" drawn on them. Explain, **God said Gideon's army was too big. Anybody who was afraid could go home.** Remove half of the figurines. Discuss the next test (drinking water at a stream) and take away most of the remaining figurines. Say, **God wanted the people to know that they would win, but not because of the number of soldiers or because they had the bravest soldiers. They would win because of the power of God.**

Now have the children be Gideon's army. Have them line up for their weapons (which you have prepared in advance). Give each child a paper towel cardboard tube with red tissue stuffed into the top (a "torch"), a brown paper lunch bag (a "clay jar") to place over the "torch flame," and a yellow sheet of paper taped into a cone shape (a "trumpet to toot"). There were no swords, no spears, and no weapons. Only God's power.

Continue, using the Bible reference and the family page text as your guide. Lead the children, at the appropriate time, to hold up their torches, crash their jars (pop their paper bags), toot on their trumpets, and shout out, **For the Lord and for Gideon!**

MOVING
Tell the children that you are going to have races, not to find who is biggest, fastest, or strongest, because those things have nothing to do with this game, just like those things had nothing to do with Gideon's army. In this race, the children are to "run" to the goal line while holding a large playground ball between their knees. No hands are allowed to hold it in place. (Try it again holding the ball between their feet.) Children who lose the ball can go after it but must return to the spot where they dropped it. This is a silly game that you play for fun rather than to win!

To play a chase game, divide the children into two "armies." The children who are the Midianites are to pretend to be sleeping. The children in Gideon's army stand quietly by until the teacher gives the signal. Then Gideon's army pretends to toot their horns, the Midianites run away, and Gideon's army chases after them.

REVIEWING
Tell the children to pretend to be in Gideon's army. You have several questions for them to answer. Give them this clue: **The first answer is "NO! Trust in the Lord!"** (Hopefully the children will catch on that this is the answer for all the questions. You may have to lead or encourage them if they don't realize it.)

Will we win the battle because Gideon is the best leader of an army? *(NO . . .)*
Will we win because we have so many soldiers? *(NO . . .)*
Will we win because we have the bravest soldiers? *(NO . . .)*
Will we win because we have the best weapons? *(NO . . .)*
When you and I have *troubles* today, do we need the most, the bravest, or the best of everything? *(NO . . .)*
When you and I have *problems* today, do we need the most, the bravest, or the best of everything? *(NO . . .)*
When you and I are *not sure* about something today, do we need the most, the bravest, or the best of everything? *(NO . . .)*

Let's talk to God in prayer: Dear Lord, when I have troubles, help me to trust in You. When I have problems, help me to trust in You. When I am worried, help me to trust in You. Help me always to "trust in the Lord"! Amen.

LIVING
Bring out Lucas the Lamb, who says, **I wish Gideon's army was here to help me with my troubles—lions and tigers and bears, oh my!** Point out that you and the children have even bigger troubles. Instead of lions, tigers, and bears, our enemies are sin, death, and the devil! But God has the best plan of all. He sent Jesus to be our leader and to win the victory. **Jesus didn't use torches and jars. How did He save us?** Hold up a cross. **Jesus did everything. Because He is true God, Jesus won the victory over sin, death, and the devil. And the most amazing thing is—He gives His victory to us!** Read 1 Corinthians 15:57. Reread the verse and shout *hooray!*

SINGING
Have a praise parade. Either sing or listen to songs of God's love. Provide each child with a flashlight to carry like the torches of light carried by Gideon's army. (You may even want to dim the lights.) Good song choices include "I'm in the Lord's Army" (*Songs Kids Love to Sing,* p. 32) or "Onward Christian Soldiers." Point out that the Lord's army is different than any other; the Lord's army doesn't fight people, it fights sin; all the power in the Lord's army is in God's hand, and He has won the victory.

CREATING
Hold up armored action figures or pictures of medieval knights in armor. Say, **The Bible tells about the armor and weapons that people have in God's army. He had Gideon's army use torches, jars, and trumpets. Listen to what the Bible tells us to use.** Read Ephesians 6:16–17. **Our weapons in the fight against sin are *faith in Jesus* and *the Word of God,* which tells us how Jesus saved us.** Give each child a black piece of paper to fold in half, representing the cover of a Bible, which has *God's Word*. To represent the *faith* we have in Jesus, provide the children with gold ribbon or gold foil paper to make a cross. Use glue sticks to attach the cross to the cover of the "Bibles." These books need something inside. Give the children copies of John 3:16 to glue inside the cover. **These are the weapons God gives to us—the message of God's Word and faith in Jesus. He has won the victory for us!**

Focus now on the word *trust*. Be sure that children understand what the word means. Give them sheets of paper on which you have printed the word *TRUST* in large letters. Have the children decorate the page using glitter pens or marking pens to trace over the letters. Also provide stickers and other items to decorate the background. **Even though you can't read the word, you know what it says. Show this to your parents. Then say to them, "Trust in the Lord!"**

CLOSING
From an open Bible read today's Bible words to remember from Psalm 96:4: **Great is the Lord and most worthy of praise.** Explain that *praise* means "to say good things about someone." Sing several praise songs that tell of the goodness and mercy of God.

8 David, the Singing Shepherd

1 Samuel 16:1–13; Psalm 23

Theme: Praise the Lord.

GATHERING

Place a large sheet of mural paper on the floor. Randomly draw little lambs on the paper. (Or make extra copies of the children's page for today, cut out the pictures of sheep, and glue those on the mural paper.) Play recordings of Christian music and suggest that the children use crayons to draw lines and designs on the mural paper that move with the music. Encourage them to sing along. Change the music frequently for a variety of tempos. As the children work, say, **Today we will hear about David, a shepherd boy who took care of sheep. As he watched the little lambs, David would often play music on his harp and sing songs to praise God.**

OPENING

Point out that last week we heard about the music of trumpets. This week we will hear about the music of harps. Explain that a harp is a stringed musical instrument. If possible, demonstrate on an autoharp; point out that people used harps then like today a person might use a guitar. Let the children make "harps" by stretching rubber bands around shoe boxes. Be sure that the rubber bands are long enough so they don't snap back sharply and injure someone. Again play recorded Christian music. Children may strum their harps for percussive (rather than tonal) sounds to accompany the recording. Say, **Today's story tells about David. He loved the Lord. He loved to make music and sing praises to God, just like you!**

LEARNING

You will need a boy volunteer to help you tell the Bible story. And you will need seven different hats (such as a cowboy hat, baseball cap, winter stocking cap, and so on). Use the Bible reference and the family page text as a guide in telling the story.

At the point in the story where Jesse's sons are brought forward to meet Samuel, have your volunteer stand up and put on a hat. Introduce him as the oldest and tallest of Jesse's sons. Samuel wondered if this son of Jesse would be the next king. But God told him this son was not the one and reminded him that God doesn't go by how a person looks. God said, "The LORD looks on the heart" (1 Samuel 16:7). Continue this pattern: the volunteer switches to a different hat, you introduce him as the next brother, and you describe him as [the most handsome, the richest, the strongest, the smartest, the best-dressed, or the bravest]. Say that Samuel wondered if that son of Jesse would be the next king. But God told him this son was not the one. God said, "The LORD looks on the heart." Then Samuel wondered if anybody was missing, so David was brought in from the fields. God said David was the one He had chosen. Ask, **Why do you think God chose David?** ("The LORD looks on the heart.") **What do you think was in David's heart?** (Faith and trust in God.) **What does God want in our hearts?** (Faith and trust in God.)

Explain that Samuel *anointed* David. **That means he poured a special, sweet-smelling lotion on David. That was a special sign that David was *chosen* by God to someday become king.** Explain that Jesus is often called the Anointed One. **Jesus, God's own Son, was *chosen* by God to become the Savior of the world. Because Jesus was *chosen* to be our Savior, and because He takes away our sins, we have been *chosen* to be called the children of God!** Point to and name each child individually as you say, **God chose you to be His child!** *Option:* You may want to sing "Child of God" (*Little Ones Sing Praise,* p. 98, available from CPH).

MOVING

Point out that sheep follow their shepherd because they trust that the shepherd knows where to go. Play Follow the Shepherd (follow the leader). Children follow in a line as you lead them around the premises. Point out that *following* can also mean *to follow a person's actions*. Continue leading children, but add motions and a variety of steps (running, hopping, walking tall and short, and so on) for them to imitate.

Later in the lesson, after you have studied Psalm 23, play Follow the Shepherd again. This time set out props along a path and explain them at each point. Place a green blanket or large green sheet of mural paper on the floor to stand for green pastures where the "sheep" can lie down to rest. Set out a blue blanket or paper to stand for the still waters where the "sheep" can pretend to drink. Place a blanket over two rows of chairs to make a dark tunnel (the valley of the shadow of death) where the sheep walk through peacefully because they fear no evil, for the good shepherd is with them. Then lead them to a table where they can sit with folded hands as you read Psalm 23:6, explaining that Jesus, our Good Shepherd, will take us to live in heaven.

REVIEWING

Display the poster picture for today's lesson. Say, **We've been talking a lot about David. But now we want to talk about someone much more important—Jesus! In some ways David and Jesus were alike, and in some ways they were very different. David was born many, many years before Jesus, but did you know that both of them were born in the little town of Bethlehem? David was the son of _____.** (Jesse.) **Jesus is the Son of _____!** (God.)

Point to today's poster picture and say, **David gathered his sheep together and cared for them.** Display the poster picture for Lesson 16 and ask, **Whom does Jesus gather together and care for?** (His people, like you and me!)

Explain that David later became king and wore a crown. **Jesus wore a different kind of crown. Look at this picture. Can you tell me about it?** Show the poster picture for Lesson 23. Jesus is wearing a crown of thorns. Explain that Jesus suffered and then died on the cross (the next poster picture). He did this to take away our sins. He did this to save us so that we can go to heaven.

Turn to the picture for Lesson 25 and say, **David sang praises to God—but Jesus IS God! He arose from the dead at Easter. Jesus has power over sin, death, and the devil. He has won the victory for us! Praise Jesus, our Lord and God!**

LIVING

Bring out Lucas the Lamb, who says that today's Bible story is one of his favorites because it talks about lambs and sheep. Use Lucas to give background information about sheep: they are timid, they easily wander off and get lost, the shepherd often knows each one of them by name, the shepherd uses his staff (walking stick) to keep the sheep in line and out of trouble, the shepherd finds places for them to eat and drink, and the shepherd faces danger to protect his flock. Continue by saying that the Bible compares God to the Good Shepherd, and we are like the sheep. Read Psalm 95:7. Then look at Psalm 23, explaining each verse and relating it to God's care for us.

SINGING

Sing "The Good Shepherd" (*Lift Little Voices,* p. 25 and on CD). If you have not yet learned the hymn "I Am Jesus' Little Lamb" (found in most hymnals available from Concordia Publishing House), begin learning the hymn now and use it as a theme song for the remainder of this course.

CREATING

Let the children make a picture of sheep in a green pasture. Give each child a light blue sheet of paper and a half sheet of bright green paper. Have them use glue sticks to attach the green paper to the bottom half of the blue. Then provide cotton balls, which children may glue to the green (grassy) portion of the page to represent sheep. Suggest that they draw legs below each puff with a black crayon.

For an additional project, give each child a sheet of white paper. Let the children paint using cotton balls clipped with a pincher clothespin (for a handle). Children may dab the puffs in a shallow dish of paint and swirl designs on paper to the rhythm of recorded music used earlier in the lesson.

CLOSING

Read another of David's songs (portions of Psalm 145). After each verse, give a sign, such as extending an open palm, to indicate that the children are to respond with the words *Praise the Lord.* Read verses 1–3, 8–9, and 15–18. Close by reading today's Bible words to remember from Psalm 23:1: **The LORD is my shepherd.**

9. King David and Mephibosheth

2 Samuel 9:1–13

Theme: Share God's loving-kindness.

GATHERING
In advance, prepare door hangers that the children can decorate. Cut white poster paper into 4 × 10-inch sections. Near the top of each rectangle, cut a slit from the side to the center, and there cut a hole that is approximately two inches in diameter. Print *God Loves You* on each door hanger (unless children are able to do this themselves). Let the children decorate these with Christian stickers and stamps. *Option:* Arrange for a field trip to a local nursing care facility and deliver the door hangers to the residents. While there, have the children sing several songs of praise to God. If a field trip is not possible, perhaps your pastor can deliver these on his visitations there. Say, **God loves us; we want to share His love with others.**

OPENING
Draw a large stick figure, adding prominent eyes, ears, feet, and hands, emphasizing that these are blessings—gifts from God to us. You may also want to sing the first stanza of "Two Little Eyes" (*Little Ones Sing Praise,* p. 36, CPH). Then point out that because we live in a troubled world, we sometimes will have problems. Sometimes our eyes, ears, feet, and hands do not work as well as God intended. But God can bless us even in the midst of our problems. Talk about the blessings a person might have even when their eyes don't work well (glasses, guide dog, braille); blessings they might have when their ears don't work well (hearing aids, sign language, surgery); blessings when their hands don't work well (medicines, physical therapy); blessings when their feet don't work well (walkers, wheelchairs). **Today's Bible story shows us that God also uses other people to bless our lives by caring for us.**

LEARNING
Display last session's poster picture. Point out that David was a young boy when he was a shepherd. As he grew older, he had a good friend named Jonathan, who was the son of King Saul. When David and Jonathan grew up, they became soldiers. And finally, after many years, David became king. Show today's poster picture and continue to tell the story, using the Bible reference and family page text as your guide. Point out that Jonathan had been very kind to David, so David wanted to show kindness to Jonathan's family. Even more so, however, David's loving-kindness was based on the loving-kindness God first showed to him. The grace and mercy of God is what empowers us too in our Christian lives. 1 John 4:9–19 says, **"This is how God showed His love among us: He sent His one and only Son into the world that we might live through Him. . . . We love because He first loved us."**

MOVING
If possible, let children explore crutches, a wheelchair, braille printing, and other means used to assist people. (Note: Children often stare at someone using these means because they are curious; becoming familiar with the items will help the children be more comfortable around them.) Emphasize that people who use these means have a different way of seeing or walking, and so on, but there are many more ways that the people are just like everyone else. For example, most children like to play and run races. Even though a child cannot see well, he can run a race with the help of a string to guide him. Set up pairs of rope or string set about waist high between the beginning and endpoint of two racing lanes. Have children run the race, holding onto the string lightly to know where to run. Another race can be run, demonstrating that you don't have to be able to hear someone say "GO" to start a race; instead, hold a bright flag high and bring it down to mark the start of the race.

Just for fun, focus on the name MEPHIBOSHETH. Print each letter of the name, all capital letters, one letter per sheet of paper. Group the children in pairs. Hold up one letter of the name at a time, and have the children lie on the floor. Have partners work together to make the shape of the letter with their whole body. (For example, the letter T would be one child stretching out in a vertical line with the other child stretching horizontally across the top.)

REVIEWING
Emphasize that any good we sinners do is based on the fact that God has created a new and clean heart in us by forgiving our sins through Jesus; and then, through the power of the Holy Spirit working through God's Word and the Sacraments, He empowers us to live a life for Him, sharing the love and forgiveness He first gave to us. Encourage the children to fill in the missing word in the following statement. **God is good to me; He leads me to be _____ to others.** Continue this pattern to stress that God initiates the action and empowers us to live for Him in all that we do as His people. Other statement possibilities: God [forgives, cares for, is kind to, loves, is honest with] me; God leads me to [forgive, care for, be kind to, love, be honest with] others, and so forth.

LIVING
Bring out Lucas the Lamb, who is wearing a sling on his arm. Have him discuss what he can and can't do because of his injury. Have him discuss what a blessing from God it is that a doctor helped him at the hospital and that his mom continues to help him. Point out that in a week Lucas's arm will be better. Sometimes God heals right away. That doesn't always happen; but God is always with us, blessing us in other ways. We can trust that He has a plan for us. Part of that plan is that, because Jesus has taken our sins away, we will someday live in heaven, where there will be no problems, troubles, or pain.

SINGING
Sing songs about sharing the love that God gives to us: sing "Love One Another" (*Lift Little Voices,* p. 41 and on CD) or "Love, Love, Love" (*Little Ones Sing Praise,* p. 30). Remind the children that God can use them to help others and be a blessing to others. Sing "Blessings" (*LLV,* p. 39) or "Jesus Wants Me for a Helper" (*LOSP,* p. 33).

CREATING
Make a wall hanging that reinforces the idea that God first loved us, and we are led by Him to love others. Give each child five 4-inch squares of colored paper. Have them draw a cross on the first square, a heart on the next, print their name (or draw a self-portrait) on the third, draw a heart on the next, and the letter U (for you) on the last one. Turn the squares over and tape a two-foot length of yarn down the center of the squares, connecting them with just a small space between them. When turned over and hung for display, the message reads, "God loves (name, who) loves you."

Also, teach children to use their hands to make hearts. Have them fold a sheet of red paper in half. With the fold to the left (like a book) have each child align one (left) hand, with the wrist just touching the bottom corner, fingers tight together and thumb tucked under, and pointing the hand toward the opposite corner (upper right). Have children loosely trace around that hand and cut it out (with the paper still folded). It will open up to a large heart shape. Children may use glue sticks to attach this to a white sheet of paper as you print the title "Helping Hands Make Happy Hearts." Provide smaller sheets of pink paper so children can make smaller hearts to place randomly in the background. Small hearts follow a similar process except that children trace around their *left thumb* to make the heart.

CLOSING
Say, **We have talked a lot today about blessings, which are God's good gifts to us.** Point out that each time we go to a church worship service, the pastor gives a blessing—His prayer that God will be with us. His words are taken right from the Bible. Read Numbers 6:24–26. Explain key words such as *gracious* and *peace.* Then say that this is also your blessing for them—it is what you pray God will do for them. Then repeat the Bible verses.

The Bible words to remember this week are from the first portion of this blessing: **"The Lord bless you and keep you"** (Numbers 6:24).

10 Elijah's Ups and Downs

1 Kings 18:16–19:18

Theme: God is near, blessing us.

GATHERING

Draw a smiley face on a paper plate and a sad face on another. Let children sort pictures cut from magazines, placing them on the plates to indicate if it makes them happy or sad. (A similar procedure can be used to sort the smells in unlidded canisters, like film canisters, which have cotton balls saturated with lemon juice, vinegar, floral perfume, onion, vanilla.) Point out that the lips turn up on the smiley face, and down on the sad face. **Our lives have happy times and sad times, we have our ups and downs, but God is always with us no matter what happens.**

OPENING

Continue the "ups and downs" concept. As you describe situations, children are to give the thumbs-up sign for a good thing, and give a thumbs-down if it is not. Suggest situations: your family is going to an amusement park; your grandmother is sick; your ice-cream cone fell on the floor; your mom fixed your favorite dessert; you fell and broke your arm; your best friend comes over to play. Give a thumbs-up sign and say, **Who is with you when things are going good?** (God is near.) **Who is with you when things are going bad?** (God is near.) **In today's Bible story, we will hear about Elijah, who had ups and downs, good times and bad times. But he found out that, no matter what happened to him, God was always near.**

LEARNING

Explain that Elijah was a prophet of God. But it was a very bad time for Elijah and other believers. (Give a thumbs-down sign.) Tell about bad King Ahab, who wanted to kill Elijah. (Thumbs-down.) Bad King Ahab had led the people to worship an idol, a false god, named Baal. (Thumbs-down.) And now for two years there had been no rain (thumbs-down) and plants and animals were dying of thirst (thumbs-down). Explain that God wanted the people to learn that only He could help them. Elijah challenged the king and the prophets of Baal to have a contest! The prophets of Baal would build an altar and pray to the statue of Baal; Elijah would build an altar and pray to the Lord. The true God would send fire from heaven. Everyone liked the plan.

Explain that the 450 prophets of the idol Baal prayed all morning and all afternoon. But nothing happened. (Thumbs-down.) Read 1 Kings 18:27 to hear how Elijah even teased and taunted them. But nothing happened. (Thumbs-down.)

After a whole day for Baal, it was finally Elijah's turn. He took 12 large stones to make an altar. He soaked the altar in water three times. And then he said a short prayer. Read the prayer in 1 Kings 18:36–37. Immediately God sent fire to burn up the sacrifice, the water, and the altar! (Thumbs-up.) **God is amazing and all-powerful. But there was more.** When Elijah's servant saw a little cloud about the size of his hand, Elijah said to hurry home because, after two years, it was going to rain, a lot! (Thumbs-up.) God gave Elijah such amazing strength that Elijah ran down the mountain faster than Ahab could go with his horses and chariot! (Thumbs-up.)

That was an amazing, upbeat, happy part of Elijah's story. But now we will see that things didn't always go well for Elijah. In fact, Elijah began to feel that he was the only one left who believed in God. He was ready to give up. The Bible tells us that Elijah said, "I have had enough, LORD" (1 Kings 19:4). (Thumbs-down.) Elijah went to a cave to be all by himself. (Place a blanket over two chairs and then crawl into your little "cave" to tell the rest of the story.) **Where was God now that Elijah needed Him?** Add facial emotions as you tell the repeating pattern of a great wind that passed by but God wasn't in it (thumbs-down), an earthquake occurred but God wasn't in it (thumbs-down), a fire roared by but God wasn't in it (thumbs-down). Then Elijah heard a still, small voice, a whisper, and it was God speaking to him. (Thumbs-up.) Elijah slowly came out of the cave. He now knew that God is with us in our ups and downs, good times and bad times, exciting and quiet times, because God never leaves us. (Thumbs-up.) To encourage Elijah, God told him that, in fact, there were seven thousand believers in the land! Praise God!

MOVING

Continue the focus on "ups and downs," but in a different way. Have three games in which the children stand in line, one behind the other, and pass a ball (either as a single line or as team relays). In the first game, the ball is passed from one person to the next, up over their heads, till it reaches the end of the line. In the second game, the first person passes the ball down, between their legs, to the next person and so on to the end of the line. The third game has ups and downs. The first person passes the ball overhead, the next person passes it between their legs, alternating this pattern.

REVIEWING

Cut out two large paper arrows (rectangles with triangle shapes to make the point). As you look at an arrow pointing up, talk about some of the good things that happened to Elijah and good things that happen in our lives. Draw a small, upward pointing arrow on the large arrow for each situation discussed. Then, on an arrow pointing down, draw downward pointing arrows for each difficult situation discussed about Elijah's life and ours. Say, **No matter what happens, in all things, God is with us.** Cut the triangles off each arrow. Reposition the pieces to make a cross—the two rectangles placed vertically, one above the other, and the triangles placed as cross arms. **Jesus is always with us, just as He promised. Jesus takes away our most difficult problems—sin, death, and the power of the devil. And because of Jesus, we will someday live with Him in heaven!**

LIVING

Bring out Lucas the Lamb, who is jumping with excitement and says, **Wow! The story of Elijah is so exciting—fire came from heaven, rain poured after two years without any, and then Elijah ran even faster than the king's horses and chariot. God was really with Elijah. But nothing exciting like that ever happens to me.** Remind Lucas about Elijah's time in the cave. God doesn't always come to us in exciting and amazing ways. God wasn't in the wind, the earthquake, or the fire. God came in a still, small voice. **God is with us during the everyday, ordinary, quiet times of our lives too. That is what is so amazing about God's love. He is always near.** Read these Bible verses: Matthew 28:20 and Psalm 121:8.

SINGING

Elijah had the contest against the prophets of Baal so that he could tell all the people about the true God. Sing "You've Got to Tell" (*Lift Little Voices*, p. 42 and on CD).

CREATING

Make a picture of Elijah's altar. Give each child at least 12 small, circular oyster soup crackers, which they can glue onto a sheet of paper, stacking them in rows one above the other, about four or five per row. Draw a red flame in the sky above the altar.

As a reminder that God is with us everywhere in all circumstances, let children cut out pictures from magazines and glue them to sheets of paper to be stapled into a booklet form. Have the children use a red marker or red crayon to draw a cross beside each picture to remind us that God is with us wherever we are—at the beach, at home, in a restaurant, in good times and bad times, during ups and downs.

CLOSING

Read what the people of Israel said when they saw the fire sent from heaven by the Lord in answer to Elijah's prayer. Read 1 Kings 18:39. Praise the Lord with the song "My God Is So Great." In addition to the traditional verse, add the following, which tells of God's most amazing act of greatness. (See *Songs Kids Love to Sing*, p. 40).

**My God loves me so, His love is so mighty,
He gave His Son, Jesus, for me.** (Repeat first two lines.)
**He died for my sins, He rose from the grave,
He'll come back in glory for me.** (Repeat first two lines.)

Copyright © 1994 Concordia Publishing House.

Close with the Bible words: **[Jesus said,] "I am with you always"** (Matthew 28:20).

11 Naaman, Listen to God's Messenger — 2 Kings 5:1–16

Theme: Trust in the Lord.

GATHERING

Set out plastic dishpans, each filled with several inches of clean sand. Spray with water misters so that the sand can be molded. Add water from pitchers to create lakes, rivers, oceans, and streams. **An important part of today's Bible story is the Jordan River.**

OPENING

In a bag place items used when taking a bath, such as a bar of soap, shampoo, washcloth, rubber duck, and so on. **This is a riddle-in-a-bag. Can you guess where you would use these things?** When the children have guessed, say, **In today's Bible story we will hear about Naaman, a man who took seven baths! Let's find out why.**

LEARNING

Give each child several red dot stickers (available at office supply stores). **You can pretend to be Naaman. He was an important army officer. But he was very sick with leprosy. He had sores all over his body. You can put the red dots on your face and arms to look like Naaman. The doctors back then had no medicines to make the sores go away. A little girl was a servant for Naaman's wife.** (Explain the work of a servant.) **The little girl said God's prophet Elisha could help him.**

Naaman traveled far with his chariot and horses to see this prophet called Elisha. Children may pretend to hold the reins of the horses as they bump along the road. Then have them knock on wood and say, **Naaman knocked on Elisha's door. But Elisha did not answer. Naaman was insulted. After all, he was an important army officer, and Elisha didn't even bother to talk to him. Elisha sent out a servant with this message, "Go wash seven times in the Jordan River." Now Naaman was really mad.** Have the children make an angry face. **Naaman said, "This is ridiculous. I'm going home. The Jordan River won't wash away my sores."**

Explain that Naaman's servants convinced him to try it—it was an easy task, and he had nothing to lose. So Naaman went to the river. Have the children move up and down as if dunking in the river seven times, while counting from 1 to 7. (Later, distribute the children's pages, and have them add the numbers 1–7 to the picture.)

When he was finished, his sores were gone. He was healed. Remove all the red dot stickers. **What had healed him? It wasn't the Jordan River; it wasn't the prophet Elijah; it WAS the promise and power of God that healed him. Naaman now trusted in God as the true God. He said, "I will worship the Lord."**

MOVING

Ask the children to do things such as take three steps backward; jump up and down four times; touch your nose and then touch your toes; twirl around once and clap twice. (Give one set of directions at a time.) Point out that listening carefully and then following the directions is important. **In our Bible story, Naaman listened to the message from the prophet. But he did not want to follow the directions he was given. Listening was not enough; he also needed to trust the message.**

In the next activity, point out that we use water for many different reasons. Hold up an object or picture, and have the children act out (pantomime) how water is used with it. For example, hold up a tall glass and they can pretend to drink water from a glass. Other items could be a bar of soap, a beach ball, a houseplant, a basket of laundry. The last item to show is a picture of a church. Say, **In our church, water is used in Baptism. The pastor pours water on a person in the name of the Father and of the Son and of the Holy Spirit. Baptism is a gift from God. The Bible tells us that in Baptism our sins are washed away because of all that Jesus has done for us. Listen to Acts 2:38, "Repent and be baptized, every one of you, in the name of Jesus Christ for the forgiveness of your sins."**

LIVING

Continue with Lucas the Lamb, who says, **Wait a minute! I don't get this. I don't understand! How can Baptism wash away my sins? I know water washes away dirt from my hands, but how can it wash away sins from my heart?** Explain that it is not the water; it is the Word and promise of God that works through the water; it is a miracle of God. Compare this to Naaman in the Jordan River; it was not the river water that healed; it was the Word and promise of God working through the water.

REVIEWING

Retell the Bible story from Naaman's point of view. Discuss each verse you read.

I listened to a little girl.
She was a common slave.
She said, "God's prophet can help you."
Her words were very brave.

But then I did not listen to
The words the prophet sent.
I was so angry and so mad.
And off I quickly went.

But then I listened once again.
This time a servant spoke,
"The task is easy. Why not try?
It is your only hope."

So to the Jordan I returned
And followed God's command.
My sickness stopped! Each sore was gone
From leg, face, foot, and hand!

God turned what's bad to something good.
I know God's truly great.
My sickness brought me to the Lord.
Let's praise God! Celebrate!

SINGING

Point out that the little servant girl trusted God's power. She was not afraid to tell people about the Lord. **God asks us to tell others about Jesus. It is an important job. It's a job for children as well as grown-ups!** Sing "You've Got to Tell" (*Lift Little Voices*, p. 42 and on CD) and "Go Tell" (*Little Ones Sing Praise*, p. 104).

CREATING

Make tools for telling the Bible story. Give each child a brown paper lunch bag. On both sides of the bag, they can make a puppet face, drawing a picture of Naaman. On one side add red dots for the leprosy sores. When they turn the bag over to the other side, the sores will be gone. Add a red heart to the second picture and say, **Naaman's sores were healed. And even more important, Naaman learned to trust in God with his whole heart.**

For another project, color the bottom half of a paper plate dark blue for the waters of the Jordan River and color the sky a lighter blue. Cut a slit about two inches wide at the center. On wooden craft sticks children may draw a face and body with red dots (Naaman with leprosy) and on the other side draw Naaman healed. From the back of the plate stick this puppet through the slit in the water, move the puppet up and down seven times as Naaman washed in the Jordan River. Then flip the stick puppet over to show his change.

CLOSING

Print 1 through 7 in large numbers on colored paper. Hold up and say each number as you count off while saying the following chant seven times.

Teacher: Do you trust the Lord?

Children: Oh, yes I do!

Then sing a stanza of "I Am Trusting You, Lord Jesus" (*Little Ones Sing Praise*, p. 24 and in many other Lutheran hymnals). Read aloud today's Bible words to remember from Psalm 52:8: **I trust in God's unfailing love for ever and ever.**

12 Jonah, Tell God's Message
Jonah 1–3

Theme: Share God's Good News.

GATHERING
Play hide-and-seek. When you stop to rest or regroup say, **In today's Bible story we will hear about a man named Jonah who tried to run away and hide from God. Do you think God found him? Why?** (God knows all things and sees all things.)

OPENING
Think about recent Bible stories you've had. **What surprising thing did God do when the people of Israel were trapped at the Red Sea?** (God separated the waters so they could cross over on dry land.) **What surprising thing did God ask of Gideon's army?** (They were not to use weapons.) **In what surprising way did God cure Naaman's leprosy?** (Naaman had to wash seven times in the Jordan River.) **The surprising thing in today's Bible story is how God used a big fish to teach Jonah a lesson. And the most surprising thing God ever did was to have His own Son, Jesus, die on a cross to save sinners! But that is how great God's love is!**

LEARNING
Have children imitate your actions as you tell the story. **God told the prophet Jonah, "Preach to the people in the city of Nineveh. Tell them to repent of their sins." God told Jonah to do it NOW!** (Point to the right in a demanding way.) **But Jonah said NO to God.** (Cross arms stubbornly.) **Jonah ran off in the other direction.** (Point to the left.) **Jonah tried, but you can't run away from God.** (Run in place.) **Instead of going to Nineveh** (point right), **Jonah took a boat to Tarshish** (point left). **As the boat sailed on the sea, God sent a terrible storm.** (Rock back and forth as if wind-tossed.) **Everyone was afraid the ship would sink and they would drown.** (Act afraid.) **Finally, Jonah said, "This is my fault. I disobeyed God. He told me to go to Nineveh NOW** (point right), **but I said NO and went the other way** (point left)." **The sailors picked up Jonah and threw him overboard, into the sea.** (Pretend to lift something heavy and toss it overboard.) **Immediately the storm stopped.** (Give the baseball back and forth "safe" sign.) **Jonah sank down, down, down.** (Hold your nose and slowly bend down.) **But God saved Jonah. God sent a great big fish that swallowed Jonah. He was in the belly of that great fish for one-two-three days!** (Count off the numbers on your fingers.) **What do you think Jonah did there for three days? He prayed to God.** (Fold your hands.) **Listen to the words of his prayer.** (Read aloud Jonah 2:1–2 and 9.) **God heard Jonah's prayer, and God rescued him. God had the fish spit Jonah out onto dry land. Once again God told Jonah to go to Nineveh NOW!** (Point right.) **Do you think Jonah said NO! Oh, no!** (Shake your head NO.) **Jonah NOW did what the Lord told him to do.** (Shake your head YES.) **Jonah went to the city of Nineveh. Jonah told the people to repent of their sins. The people listened. They were sorry they had sinned. Even their king was sorry and prayed to the Lord. God heard their prayers and forgave the people.** (Fold your hands and have the children pray with you.) **Dear God, we are like Jonah and the people of Nineveh. We have sinned and we are sorry. Forgive us for the sake of Jesus our Savior. Amen.**

MOVING
Play a running game that goes in two different directions. When you shout out *Nineveh,* point to your right and the children are to run in that direction. When you shout out *Tarshish,* point to your left and children are to run in that direction. Vary your tempo, sometimes switching directions faster than other times.

Then play Throw-Jonah-Overboard. Use a washable marker to draw a stick man on a ball to represent Jonah. Toss him into a bucket with a fish drawn on it. Put two lines of masking tape on the floor to mark where the ball-throwers and the bucket-catchers stand. As children improve in skill, increase the distance between the lines.

REVIEWING
Say, **We've learned several things from the story of Jonah: God knows all things, God often does surprising things, God hears our prayers, and God is ready to forgive. But there is one more lesson to talk about. We need to know why God insisted that Jonah go to Nineveh and why Jonah didn't want to go. The people of Nineveh were Jonah's enemies. Jonah did not want his enemies to have God's love and forgiveness. But he was wrong. The Bible, in 1 Timothy 2:3–4, says, "God our Savior . . . wants all men [people] to be saved and to come to a knowledge of the truth." God asked Jonah to tell people about God's love and forgiveness. God asks you and me to do the same. Whom can you tell? Start by talking to your own family about what you know about Jesus.** Have the children make a tool to use. Provide a paper towel cardboard tube for each child. Attach strips of precut colored paper to the tube so that the bottom ⅓ is orange, the middle ⅓ is red, and the top is left as is. Use black markers to draw a sad face on the top section, the cross of Jesus on the red section, and a stick figure of a person with arms raised in celebration on the orange section. Say, **You can use this tube to tell about Jesus. Start at the top with the sad color and sad face. This reminds us that we are sinners. We disobey God's will. The next section is red to remind us of the love of God, who sent Jesus to die on the cross to take away our sins. The bottom section shows a happy color and a happy person because we are forgiven and saved. We have the joy of the Lord!**

LIVING
Have Lucas the Lamb show several items that have the Christian fish symbol on them. (Note: Children will not understand the Greek *ichthys* symbolism, so use this other interpretation to help them begin to connect the fish symbol with Christianity.) Lucas says, **I saw a fish picture in church too. Is this "Jonah's fish"?** You respond, **Actually this reminds us of Jesus. Jonah was inside a fish for three days. But after Jesus died on the cross, He was in the *grave* for three days. Jesus is true God with power over death. So on the third day, Easter, Jesus came alive again!**

SINGING
Say, **Jonah found out that you can't run away from God. Actually, we can be very happy about that because nothing can ever separate us from God and His loving-kindness and forgiveness.** Sing a reminder of this: "Nothing Can Keep Us" (*Lift Little Voices,* p. 43 and on CD).

CREATING
This art project ties in with the "Living" section of the lesson. Have the children draw a picture of a fish made from a large circle for the body and a slightly smaller-sized square for the tail. Use scissors to cut out the shape. Draw an eye and a smile on the fish; draw horizontal lines on the tail to make it look like a fin; draw a stick-figure Jonah in the belly of the fish. Turn the shape over and make an Easter picture by coloring the circle gray for the stone that was rolled away. Color the square yellow with a robed stick figure of Jesus coming out of the tomb, alive in all His glory. **Jesus died on the cross and was in the grave for three days, and then He arose!**

For another fish activity, give each child a brown paper bag, flattened and horizontal. The bag opening will become tail fins, so on the opposite end draw an eye and a smile. Add fish scales to the body, making large "C" shapes in a variety of colors. Stuff the fish with crumpled newspaper. Use string to tie the bag shut about two or three inches from the opening. Fan out the back end of the fish to look like tail fins.

CLOSING
Sing "You've Got to Tell" (*Lift Little Voices,* p. 42 and on CD) or this song, using the melody of "Are You Sleeping." Have the children echo each phrase you sing.

Tell God's message. (repeat)
Share His love. (repeat)
Tell the world the Good News (repeat)
From above. (repeat)

Close by reading these Bible words to remember from Psalm 145:8: **The Lord is . . . slow to anger and rich in love.** Because of His rich love, God pursued both Jonah and the people of Nineveh to bring them to repentance and salvation.

13 Three Men Stay Standing   *Daniel 3*

Theme: Honor God above all.

GATHERING
Lead the children in using drums to strike the number of counts (syllables) in their own names (such as Cyn-thi-a). In the same way, become familiar with today's Bible names (Shadrach, Meshach, Abednego, Nebuchadnezzar), repeating them frequently.

OPENING
Play Teacher, May I? Children line up on one side of the room and try to reach the other side of the room. The teacher says, **Children, you may take one giant step forward.** The children respond, *Teacher, may I?* The teacher then says yes, and the children may progress. Choices of "steps" may include steps forward or backward, giant or baby steps, scissor steps, hopping steps, and so on. Everyone should be able to reach the other side about the same time. Then be seated and say, **In this game you obeyed my command. Let's hear a Bible story in which three young men had to choose between obeying the king's command and obeying God's command.**

LEARNING
Set out about a dozen clothespin puppets made by drawing faces on the round part of the clothespin and sticking the "legs" of the clothespin into a play-dough base so each will stand. Explain that many people of Israel had been taken from their homes by their enemies and were forced to live in this faraway land. Three of these people were young men named Shadrach, Meshach, and Abednego. They listened to God's Word and trusted the Lord to help them. Set out three more clothespin puppets. Distinguish these three by painting the body of their clothespins red or blue. Set out a clothespin puppet that wears a robe (a square of fabric glued to the back of the pin) and has a crown on its head cut from yellow paper. Explain that the king of Babylon was a powerful and proud man named Nebuchadnezzar. The king ordered a statue to be built that was about as tall as an eight-story building. Set out a "Ken" doll (or large action figure) that is completely covered and molded with aluminum foil to represent the statue. An announcement was made that when the music played, everyone was to bow down and worship the king's statue. Whoever did not obey would die in a fiery furnace. Blow a horn of some kind and tip all the clothespin people flat to the ground except for the three young men. Point out that it was easy to see who did not obey the king because they were the only ones standing. But they chose to obey God rather than the king. Talk about the anger of the king, especially when the three men said that God could help them, and even if God chose not to help, they would faithfully trust that God knows what is best. They knew that God would take them to heaven if they died. Set out a shoe box covered inside and out with red paper and tipped over on its side. Place the three men in the fiery furnace and then add the angel of the Lord (a Christmas angel figurine or a clothespin puppet wrapped in white fabric). Conclude with the remarkable ending of the three men still standing in the furnace, joined by God's angel, and then coming out unharmed as the king recognized God's power.

MOVING
Play a variation of Duck-Duck-Goose. Have one person be "it" while the rest sit in a circle on the floor. "It" walks around, touching each person on the head, calling out either *Shadrach, Meshach,* or *Abednego*. When "it" touches a person and says *Nebuchadnezzar,* this chosen person stands up, chases "it" and tries to tag her, while "it" tries to run around the circle and return to the spot where *Nebuchadnezzar* was sitting. Whatever the result, *Nebuchadnezzar* becomes the next person who is "it."

Before playing the next game ask, **What happened in the Bible story when the music played?** (People were supposed to bow down to the statue.) **We are going to play a game with music for a different purpose. When the music plays** (a taped recording), **walk around this circle of chairs. When the music stops, quickly sit down. Be quick! There are not enough chairs for everyone.** Each time, several people will be left standing. Continue, letting all children play each time.

REVIEWING
Distribute the children's pages, noting that nothing is missing, but there is something extra to add. Say, **Why did Shadrach, Meshach, and Abednego do what they did? It wasn't because they were scared of the king or the fiery furnace. They knew this promise of God: "Call upon Me in the day of trouble; I will deliver you, and you will honor Me" (Psalm 50:15). God's love in their hearts was leading them.** Have the children add hearts to the pictures of the three men. Then read this poem.

The royal command said, "Bow down low
Or into the furnace you will go."
But look, three men were still standing.
What made them brave? Read aloud Deuteronomy 31:6.

Before the king, the men had to stand.
But they felt safely held in God's hand.
So all three men kept on standing.
What promise did they trust? Read aloud Isaiah 41:13.

Into the fire the three men were thrown.
But now God's great pow'r to all was known,
For now FOUR men were still standing.
And one was the angel of God! Read aloud Psalm 91:11–12.

LIVING
Bring out Lucas the Lamb, who says he understands how Shadrach, Meshach, and Abednego felt when the mean king commanded them to do something that was wrong. Lucas says there is a mean neighborhood kid who wanted him to throw stones at the windows of an empty house. Lucas knew that was wrong and chose to obey God's will. The mean kid laughed at Lucas and called him a chicken. Lucas got angry and shouted, "I am not a chicken. I am a lamb." Then the mean kid threw stones at Lucas. It was very difficult, but Lucas prayed to God. He asked God to forgive him for getting angry, and he asked God to make him strong in faith to obey the Lord. Discuss similar situations in everyday life, emphasizing that God leads us to follow His way through His Word. He forgives us through Jesus when we are weak and sinful, and He strengthens us through the Holy Spirit.

SINGING
Sing "Nothing Can Keep Us" (*Lift Little Voices*, p. 43 and on CD). Add a third stanza, repeating three times: *fiery furnaces and mean old kings*. You may also want to sing "Listen to the Stories" (*LLV,* p. 9), stanzas 1, 3, 5, and 7.

CREATING
Point out that the fire in the Bible story was very dangerous. But now you will make beautiful pictures of fire. **Fire can also be a good thing, like in a fireplace that makes the house warm on a cold night.** Give each child a sheet of white paper and squares of yellow, red, and orange tissue paper. Tear the colored tissue paper into long strips and place them randomly on the white sheet to look like fiery flames. Then give the children small bowls partly filled with a mixture of equal amounts of water and white glue. Dip paintbrushes in this mixture and paint it over the tissue flames.

In another activity, recall the music made with drums earlier in the session and the horns that were blown in the Bible story. Make musical shakers by placing breakfast cereal into small, unfilled potato-chip cans. Fill the cans no more than ⅓ full, seal the lids with strong tape, and decorate the outside of the containers with paper, stickers, and other trim. **Nebuchadnezzar used music to make people disobey God. We can use musical instruments in a different way—to praise God! Listen to Psalm 150 in the Bible. It mentions many musical instruments. Every time I say the word *praise*, shake the instruments you just made.**

CLOSING
Speak the song "Prayer" (*Lift Little Voices*, p. 49) as a closing prayer. Then from an open Bible read today's words to remember from Ephesians 6:10: **Be strong in the Lord and in His mighty power.**

14 Angels and Shepherds Praise

Luke 2:1–20

Theme: Give glory to Jesus, our Savior.

GATHERING

Set out Christmas cards and decorations to sort. Let children separate out those that are about the birth of Jesus—the true meaning of Christmas. **Those other things are pretty or fun, but they do not tell the real Christmas story. We celebrate Christmas because Jesus, true God, came to take away our sins.**

OPENING

Say, **Christmas is the day Jesus was born. It is His birthday!** Sing "Happy Birthday" using the traditional tune. **At Jesus' birthday, there was singing, but not the song we just sang. Listen closely to God's Word in the Bible to find out who sang what song.**

LEARNING

You will need a nativity scene and several other items mentioned in this narrative. Read Luke 2:1–20, stopping to add comments as indicated.

Luke 2:1—Explain that Caesar Augustus was the Roman emperor—a powerful ruler over many, many countries.

Luke 2:2–3—Explain that Caesar wanted to know the number of people in all his lands. So everyone had to be registered and counted. Register and count the children by printing a mark on the top of each one's hand, using a stamp and ink pad.

Luke 2:4—Show today's poster page and point to the little town of Bethlehem. Explain that Bethlehem was also called the city of David because this was the town where David, the shepherd boy and king, had lived many years before this.

Luke 2:5–6—Mary was about to have a baby, just as the angel had told her. An angel had told Joseph that the baby should be named *Jesus,* because He would save the people from their sins. Display the Mary and Joseph figures from the nativity scene.

Luke 2:7—Bring out the stable and explain that it was a barn, the only place they could stay that night because the inn (hotel) was already filled. Set out the baby Jesus in a manger and explain that a manger was actually a food box for animals that ate straw and hay. Add animals to the scene. Hold up a long, white strip of fabric. Explain that in those days swaddling cloths were wrapped around a baby instead of using diapers and a baby blanket. Sing "Away in a Manger."

Luke 2:8–9—Some distance away take out a shepherd and sheep figurines. Add an angel. Explain that the shepherds were terrified at the angel's sudden brightness shining all around them. They had never seen anything like it before.

Luke 2:10–12—The angel's message was good news for all people of the world. The angel called Jesus *Savior* (He would save us from sin), *Christ* (the Chosen One promised by God), and *Lord* (true God, not just a human baby). The angel told exactly how to find Jesus; today, the Bible tells us exactly about Jesus our Savior.

Luke 2:13–14—Remind children that angels are the messengers of God who serve Him and who also sing His praises. Here they sang the "birthday song" for Jesus.

Luke 2:15–16—The shepherds didn't wonder or wait. They hurried to see the Savior and worshiped Him. Rush the shepherd and sheep figurines to the stable.

Luke 2:17–20—The shepherds had a busy night: they told everyone they saw about the birth of the Savior, and then as they returned to their sheep, they praised God.

MOVING

Play a variation of pin the tail on the donkey. Display a large hillside scene drawn on mural paper. It can be simple green grass below and dark blue sky above, or use the poster picture or a Christmas card as your guide. Blindfold a child with a scarf and give him an angel sticker (or angel picture with tape on the back). Gently guide the child to the mural and let him place the angel in the sky. When each child has had a turn, you will have a picture of a choir of angels.

In another game, set up a running area with one line representing Bethlehem and the other line for the hills outside of town. All the children are shepherds, who start on the hills outside of town. When you say, **Shepherds, run to Bethlehem,** the children run to the other line. When you say, **Shepherds, return to your flocks,** the children walk back to the hills, but they talk to as many other children as they can, saying, **The Savior is born!** Repeat this pattern several times.

REVIEWING

Use this simple but unique way to review the Christmas story. Display a large sheet of white mural paper set horizontally. Draw a large hill extending across the top of the page. About 1/3 of the way from the bottom of the page draw the ground line. On the right half of this line draw four small buildings; three are square-shaped houses with a door and a window; the fourth is a simple stable, with pointed roof and a manger. As you retell the story, use a red marker or red paint to draw Mary and Joseph's path as they come over the right side of the hill from Nazareth. Continue the path, making an arrow pointing to each of the three houses where there was no room for them, and then finally an arrow pointing to the stable.

Now switch to the color yellow. On the left half of the page draw a large yellow arrow pointing down from heaven to the hillside to represent the angel who brought good news. Then draw many yellow arrows pointing down for the choir of angels.

Switch to the color green for the shepherds. Draw a line from the hillside on the left directly to the stable. Then, to show the shepherds telling people about Jesus on their way home, draw an arrow from the stable to each house, in turn, and then to the hill.

LIVING

Bring out Lucas the Lamb wearing a gold garland that encircles the top of his head. Lucas says every year when they act out the Christmas story, he has to play the part of a lamb. **But this year I want to be an angel! See my halo? I want to sing glory to God!** Comment that this is a good idea and ask the children to join Lucas. Give each child a gold garland halo to wear, and continue with the next section.

SINGING

Sing the refrains of songs that tell the angels' message, such as "Glory to God" (*Lift Little Voices,* p. 12 and on CD) and "Angels We Have Heard on High." (Point out that *Gloria in excelsis Deo* are words from another language that mean *Glory to God in the Highest,* the song of the angels!)

CREATING

Provide plenty of materials so children can complete more than one of these angel projects. Make an angel by turning a white plastic spoon upside down. The handle becomes the body of the angel and the portion of the spoon that curves outward is the angel face. Use fine-tip markers to draw a face on the spoon. Strips of yellow or brown yarn can be glued in place for hair. To make angel wings, accordion-fold a square of white paper (or gold wrapping paper) back and forth. Wrap tape around the center to hold the wings in place. The wings can be attached at the back of the spoon handle with a tape roll.

Another type of angel can be made on white paper by drawing two circles—one large and one small. (Provide cardboard patterns or plastic jar lids that children can trace around.) Cut out both circles. Cut the bigger circle in half across the middle. The bottom half of the circle will be the angel's body; tape or glue it to a colorful sheet of paper. Then glue the smaller circle in place as the angel's head. Cut the remaining piece in half, down the center. Position these two pieces as angel wings, gluing the pointed end at the angel's "neck" and the rest of the wing fanning up and out. *Option:* Print *Glory to God* on each picture, perhaps using a glittery gold crayon or glitter pen.

CLOSING

Emphasize why the birth of Jesus is so important: He is true God, who came to take away our sins. Read John 3:16 and then sing the song based on that Bible verse, "God So Loved the World" (*Lift Little Voices,* p. 33 and on CD). Close by reading aloud the important message of the angel, spoken to the shepherds and also to you and me: **"Today . . . a Savior has been born to you; He is Christ the Lord" (Luke 2:11).**

15 Simeon and Anna Meet Baby Jesus
Luke 2:21–40

Theme: God keeps His promises.

GATHERING
Let the children practice things that occur in church. Set up rows of benches or chairs; let "ushers" pass out old service bulletins; while holding hymnals, sing together a hymn they know; say a familiar Bible verse while holding an open Bible. Talk about what happens in church. Say, **Today we will hear about Jesus going to church when He was just a baby. Mary and Joseph took baby Jesus to the temple—a very large church—in Jerusalem.**

OPENING
Set out a gift-wrapped box. Tell the children that there is something inside it for them, but they will have to wait until you say the time is right to open it. (Place stickers or a treat for each child in the box; do not open it until later in the lesson.) Point out that waiting is hard to do; sometimes it seems like we will have to wait forever. **The people in our Bible story had been waiting a long time for God to keep His promise. They waited year after year. It was hard to wait. But they trusted that God would keep His promise. God always does!**

LEARNING
Use the Bible reference and family page as your guide in telling the Bible story. Display the poster page and point out that Mary and Joseph brought baby Jesus to the temple-church. **This is God's will. God also wants your parents to bring you to church.** Point to Simeon and say, **God had told Simeon he would not die before seeing the Savior. When Simeon saw baby Jesus, he knew right away who Jesus was. God had kept His promise to Simeon. But even more important, God had kept His promise to the whole world. That is why Jesus is called the Promised Savior. All people who believe in Him have forgiveness and eternal life. That is God's promise to us. And God keeps all His promises. Listen to the words of thanks Simeon said as he held baby Jesus.** Hold an open Bible and read Luke 2:29–30. **Jesus is our salvation—our Savior, who saves us from sin, death, and the power of the devil.** Then point to Anna and explain that she was 84 years old. She too was joyful and gave thanks to God when she saw baby Jesus. The Bible tells us she told all the people she saw that the Savior had come. **Mary and Joseph were amazed at all that happened. Once again they saw how special this baby was—God's gift of salvation to the whole world!** Distribute the children's pages and have the children draw the baby Jesus.

MOVING
If possible, invite several elderly people to stop by and play with the children as they take a break. Avoid strenuous running. Perhaps throw and catch balls or play a freeze or statue tag (where you are safe from being tagged if you freeze in position). Comment on the fact that in today's Bible story, there were people of all ages—baby Jesus, grown-ups Mary and Joseph, and elderly Simeon and Anna. **God loves people of all ages. He desires that we show love to all people—those who are the same age, those who are younger, and those who are older than we are.** If the children have waited long enough, this may be a good time to open the gift-wrapped box. Have your guests pass out the treats.

REVIEWING
Say, **You had to wait many minutes to get the treat I promised you. The people in Bible times had to wait much longer for God's promise. They had to wait hundreds and thousands of years!** (Children won't understand the numerical significance. But they will understand the tone of awe and amazement in your voice.) **God first promised the Savior to Adam and Eve because they were the first people to need that promise. But God waited to send the Savior until it was the right time. In the meantime, God repeated His promise. God told Abraham, Isaac, and Jacob that through the Savior, all nations of the world would be blessed. Year after year the people waited. God sent prophets to remind them of His promises and to tell the people more about the Promised Savior. Listen to the words of the prophet Micah, who said the Savior would be born in Bethlehem.** (Read Micah 5:2.) **And listen to the words of the prophet Isaiah, who lived hundreds of years before Jesus was born.** (Read Isaiah 7:14 and 9:6.) **The people had to wait a long, long time. But God is faithful to all His promises. Like Simeon, we can be so thankful the wait is over. We know Jesus our Savior and all He did to save us. We know that Jesus died on the cross to take away our sins and arose at Easter so we can be certain of eternal life. Like Simeon, we can say, "My eyes have seen Your salvation"** (Luke 2:30)!

LIVING
Bring out Lucas the Lamb, who is crying. Ask what is wrong and have him tell you he is sad because his friend Gertrude broke her promise. She promised she would come over to play; but now she can't because she is sick. And his friend Chadsworth promised to come over; but he said he would rather play with Edward than with Lucas. Talk about the fact that people often break their promises—sometimes they can't help it, like Gertrude, and sometimes they are unkind like Chadsworth. **But here is good news for us: God always keeps His promises. He is not like us weak and sinful people. God has always been faithful and He will continue to be faithful. Listen to what the Bible tells about God's promises: "You know with all your heart and soul that not one of all the good promises the LORD your God gave you has failed. Every promise has been fulfilled"** (Joshua 23:14). **Praise God!**

SINGING
Sing about the promise God kept when Jesus was born. Sing "God Made a Promise" (*Lift Little Voices*, p. 10 and on CD). Change the second stanza to the following:

We know God will keep His promises. (Repeat twice.)
God will keep His promises.

You may also want to sing "Ring the Bells" (*LLV*, p. 14), which celebrates, along with Simeon and Anna, that Jesus the Savior is born.

CREATING
Make pictures of Simeon and Anna. Children may draw simple circle faces with eyes and a mouth. Then provide popped popcorn, which the children may glue on the pictures to give Anna white hair and Simeon a white beard. Talk with the children about what they like about older people. **God loves older people too. God gave Anna and Simeon a very special blessing. They got to see the baby Jesus. We will see Jesus too someday in heaven. God's Word promises us that!**

Point out that the temple-church in today's Bible story was a beautiful building with tall pillars, shiny brass decorations, and colorful curtains. **Our church is beautiful too because we want to give our best to honor our Lord God.** Talk about stained-glass windows that we often see in churches today. If possible, look at those in your sanctuary or show pictures of them (perhaps from a church supply catalogue). Let the children make beautiful church windows. Give each child a sheet of paper that you have trimmed at the top to make a pointed arch. Children are to tear colored tissue paper into swatches and glue them on the paper with a half-water and half-white-glue mixture that can be applied with paintbrushes. Encourage children to overlap colors and fill the page.

CLOSING
Listen to this Bible verse about Jesus as a little child. Read Luke 2:40. **This is my prayer for each of you—that God will bless you as you grow taller and stronger, that God will make you wiser and smarter, and that the grace and love of God will always be with you.** Read Luke 2:40 again, reminding the children again that this is your prayer for them. Then, from an open Bible read today's words to remember from Hebrews 10:36: **"You will receive what [God] has promised."** These words assure us that we can trust the promises of God to be with us, to care for us, to forgive us, and to take us to heaven. **This isn't something we hope or wish for; we are sure this will happen because God keeps His promises!**

16 Jesus Welcomes Children
Mark 10:13–16

Theme: Jesus loves children.

GATHERING
Set out a large sheet of mural paper. Place a picture of Jesus at the center. Have the children dip heart-shaped, people-shaped, and/or cross-shaped cookie cutters into shallow pans of red or yellow paint, and then print these on the paper, randomly around the picture of Jesus. Add the title "Jesus Loves All People." Hang this up in a hallway where congregational members can see it.

OPENING
Ask the children how old they are. Then ask, **How old would you like to be? Why?** Let the children share ideas. Talk about how old a person needs to be in order to drive a car or vote in an election. **There are some things that you have to wait till you are older to do. Some of Jesus' disciples thought children were not old enough to see Jesus. Let's find out what Jesus thinks about little children, just like you.**

LEARNING
Read the story directly from the Bible and add comments. Read Mark 10:1 and then say, **Jesus and His disciples were walking from town to town on their way to Jerusalem. When mothers heard Jesus was near, they stopped their cooking. When fathers heard Jesus was near, they put down their hammers or fishnets. The parents took their children to see Jesus. They wanted their children to know about the Savior.** Read Mark 10:13. **But the disciples were very grouchy. They rebuked or scolded the parents and children. The disciples thought Jesus was too busy to have time for children. Or they thought Jesus was too important to be bothered with children. Or they thought Jesus was too tired and the children would not give Him rest. The moms and dads and children must have felt so sad as they walked away. But . . .** Read Mark 10:14–15. **Jesus turned things around. He was upset with the disciples. Jesus said He wanted to see the children. Jesus loves children. You are important to Jesus. He is never too busy or too tired for you.** Read Mark 10:16. **Jesus didn't just talk to the children, He held them and hugged them. Jesus blessed the children. He spoke of the good gifts of God He wanted in their lives. I want to give each of you a blessing. I want to tell you about the good gifts of God I pray for in your lives.** Go around the group, put your hand on the head of each child, say the child's name, and then give a blessing such as *may God give you joy* or *may God bless you with His love*. Then distribute copies of the reproducible page and have the children add pictures of themselves to the picture of Jesus and the children.

MOVING
Invite the pastor into your room. Explain that the pastor is one of God's helpers because he tells us about Jesus, our Savior. Have the pastor sit on the floor as the children hold hands in a circle around him. As the children walk around the circle, with the pastor in the center, they can sing "Jesus Loves the Little Children" (*LOSP*, p. 94). Then the children may sit down. Have the pastor go around the circle, placing his hand on each child and giving each a blessing.

For another activity, provide either a purchased bubble solution or make your own using dish soap and a little water. In addition to bubble wands, provide juice cans with both ends removed (tape over any rough edges) to dip in the solution. To prevent soap in the eyes, have children wave the wands and cans instead of blowing through them. Sing "Love in a Box" (*Little Ones Sing Praise*, p. 35), emphasizing the love of God that comes "a-bubbling through."

REVIEWING
Make a double-sided stoplight sign—a tall rectangle with three circles on each side. On one side the bottom circle is green, on the other side the top circle is red. All other circles are blank.

Show the green circle. **GO! Families were going to see Jesus. They were happy because they knew that Jesus is true God, who came to be their Savior.**

Show the red circle. **STOP! The disciples stopped them. The disciples said, "Don't let the little children bother Jesus."**

Show the red circle again. **STOP! Jesus stopped His disciples! Jesus wanted to see the children. Jesus always has time for children because He loves them.**

Show the green circle. **GO! Now the children could go to Jesus. He held them in His arms and blessed them.**

Show the green circle again. **GO! This message is for you! Go to Jesus in prayer. Hear His blessings of grace and forgiveness in God's Word. Jesus welcomes you!**

Hold an open Bible and say, **God's Word tells us in Romans 8:16, "We are God's children!"** Set the Bible down and say, **Jesus died on the cross and arose at Easter to save us. He takes away our sins and makes us children of God!**

LIVING
Bring out Lucas the Lamb, who says that he likes this Bible story. The children running to be with Jesus remind him of sheep running to be with their shepherd. **That's why we call Jesus the Good Shepherd!** Read John 10:14 and 27. **And you are the sheep and lambs of Jesus, the Good Shepherd!** Sing "I Am Jesus' Little Lamb."

SINGING
Listen to the song "Walking, Walking to See Jesus" (*Lift Little Voices*, p. 23 and on CD). This song retells today's Bible story. Then act out the Bible story, using the song as the narration.

CREATING
Make "Jesus Loves Me" necklaces. In advance, cut a length of yarn for each child. Tip one end of the yarn by wrapping it with a small piece of clear tape or dipping the end into white glue and letting it dry. Children are to string tubular pasta on the yarn string. Provide pasta that comes in various colors—plain yellow, tomato red, and pesto green. Children may then apply a sticker picture of Jesus to a two-inch circle of poster paper on which you have prepunched two holes to string yarn through. Children are to print their names or draw their portrait on the back. Then they are to add more tubes of pasta to complete the necklaces, which can then be tied around their necks.

Also make "I Love Jesus" headbands. Give each child a strip of colored paper to make a headband. Children may use a dark marker to draw alternating hearts and crosses on the strip. Staple each headband to fit each individual. Say, **When you wear your headbands, people can see the message that you love Jesus too.**

CLOSING
Hold up a large circle of poster paper on which you have made a large slash sign (circle with a diagonal line through it). Explain that this sign means **DON'T**. The sign might mean don't drink the water, or don't cross the street, or don't open the door. **This sign reminds me of Jesus' disciples. They said, "Don't let the children bother Jesus." But we can be thankful that Jesus loves little children like you. And He loves older people like Anna and Simeon from our last Bible story. In fact, Jesus loves everyone. He even loves sinners! We can be very, very glad about that because we are sinners and we need God's love and forgiveness. Listen to what the Bible tells us: "God demonstrates His own love for us in this: While we were still sinners, Christ died for us" (Romans 5:8). So let's change this DON'T sign and make it a sign of God's love.** Turn the circle so the line is vertical and then use a marker to add a horizontal line to make a cross. **Jesus showed His great love for us by taking away our sins on the cross and making us children of God.** Close by reading today's Bible verse, **"We are God's children"** (Romans 8:16)!

17 Jesus Heals Ten Sick Men
Luke 17:11–19

Theme: Jesus heals.

GATHERING
Set out a toy doctor kit and let the children explore the various items. Encourage them to talk about how the items are used or about any medical experiences they have had.

OPENING
Say, **God blesses us with doctors and nurses who help us when we are sick or injured. Who else helps you when you are sick or hurt?** Listen to their comments, but focus on moms and dads. Lead the children in a prayer to thank God for these people who help them.

Then ask the children if they have ever had an upset stomach and thrown up. Say, **Oh, that is so yucky and gross. But I'm sure your mom or dad helped you anyway and cleaned things up. Why would they do such a thing?** (Because they love and care for you.) **In our Bible story Jesus helps some people that no one else could or would help. There were 10 men with leprosy. They had awful sores all over their bodies. Most people would not even walk near them or touch them. They had to live outside of town, away from other people so no one would catch their disease. They had dirty, ragged clothes because no one would give them a job to earn money. They were either homeless or lived in caves. But Jesus loved them and cared about them and helped them. He was the only one who could.**

LEARNING
In advance, prepare a puppet stage, cutting off the lid of a plastic egg carton and also cutting away two of the egg cups. Make 10 puppets from wooden craft sticks by drawing a sad face at the top of each stick and red dots all over (leprosy sores). Turn one of the sticks over and draw a happy face with no dots. Turn the egg carton over and poke a stick puppet into each egg cup so that you see 10 sad faces. As you tell the Bible story, count off the 10 men. When Jesus tells them to go show themselves to the priest in Jerusalem, turn the puppet stage around and move it away. Comment that now we see the sores are gone! They have been healed! But note that one man has turned around. Bring the smiling-faced puppet toward you as you set the other puppets further away. Discuss how just one man came back to thank Jesus. Distribute the children's pages and ask what is missing. (The nine men who ran on into the city.) Let the children draw nine stick figures in the distance who are running off. Now would be a good time to bring out Lucas the Lamb. (See the "Living" section.)

MOVING
The men in the Bible story ran off to the temple-church in Jerusalem. There the priest would see that their sores were gone, and they would be able to return to their homes and jobs and a normal life. Say, **They probably ran to the temple-church. We are going to take a walking trip to the church.** Have the children count how many steps it takes to walk from the back of the church to the altar, from the front bench (pew) to the baptismal font, and other "counting trips" as you explore the area together.

Play a game of 10. Set up two relay teams at a starting line. Distribute 10 bean bags to each team. (Some children may have to run twice.) Set out a basket or bucket. At a signal, the first team members run to the bucket and toss in the bags, then return to tag the next runners. The first team to get all 10 of their bags in the bucket wins.

REVIEWING
In advance, cut out the outline of a person (gingerbread boy style) from mural paper. On the body write sins that children might do. Over each one of these attach a red paper circle with a tape roll. You will read the words aloud so they do not need to be very large. Possible phrases include: hit my friend, said mean things, disobeyed dad, messed up my room, had a temper fit, made my sister cry, and so on. Display the mural and say he is one of the 10 men with leprosy. Ask questions about the story such as: What was wrong with the man? How was he healed? Why did Jesus do that? How could Jesus do that? How do you think the man felt when he saw that his sores were gone? **He must have celebrated that now he had a new life.**

Then say that the man actually had a worse problem. And we have the same problem! **That problem is sin. We are covered with sinfulness.** Take off one red dot at a time, and read the statements to the children. Ask, **How can we get rid of those spots of sin?** (Through Jesus, who died on the cross to take them away.) **Why would Jesus do that?** (Because He loves us.) Turn the shape of the person over and ask, **How do you feel knowing that your sins are gone because Jesus took them away? Jesus gives us a new life too—we live now as children of God!**

LIVING
Bring out Lucas the Lamb, who is crying. Ask him what is wrong. Lucas says, **I'm so sad because I'm just like those nine men who ran off. Sometimes I get so excited when something good happens, I just forget to thank God. Boo-hoo! I am so sorry.** Explain to Lucas that God understands that we make mistakes, we are forgetful, and sometimes we are even unthankful. But God is always ready to forgive. It's never too late to tell Jesus we are sorry, and it's never too late to thank Him for all the blessings He gives. Join in a prayer asking Jesus to forgive unthankfulness and thanking Him for taking away our sins and making us children of God.

SINGING
Say, **The power of God to heal our sicknesses is great. The power of God to heal our sin-sickness is even greater! God loves us so much, He sent Jesus to save us for life everlasting where we will live with Him in heaven.** Sing about this in "God So Loved the World" (*Lift Little Voices,* p. 33 and on CD). You might also sing or read as a prayer the second stanza of "Prayer" (*Lift Little Voices,* p. 49). **These words remind us that God loves all people—old people, young people, sick people, well people, sinners (and that includes everybody). God loves us all and sent Jesus to save us. By faith in Him we have forgiveness, life, and salvation!**

CREATING
Point out that the 10 men in the Bible story called out to Jesus, praying, "Jesus, Master, have pity on us!" Jesus heard their prayers and answered them. Jesus hears our prayers too. We can be certain that He will answer. It might not be when we want or in the way we want it. But we can be certain that He knows what is best and that He is with us, blessing us at all times. God also leads us to pray for the needs of others. Have the children make a prayer request clip to place on their refrigerators at home. Let them use marking pens to decorate pincher clothespins. Attach a piece of magnetic tape to the back of each clothespin. Ask each child whom they would like to pray for, print the name of that person on a 3×5-inch card, and have the child draw a picture of that person. Place the card in the pincher pin. Suggest that the children ask their parents to add other names to the list and pray together for the people.

As we've been learning, Jesus loves all people. Make a special cross as a reminder of that. Each child will need two large wooden craft sticks. Glue the sticks together to make a cross. Then give each child about 10 puzzle pieces from a large "grown-up" puzzle. Use shapes that have a round "head" and "arms" sticking out (maybe arms *and* legs). (Most puzzle pieces have these shapes.) On the colorful side of the puzzle pieces, draw eyes and a smile on each head. Glue these unusual people shapes to the cross. **Remember, Jesus loves all people, of every color, size, and shape. He died on the cross to save the people of the world.**

CLOSING
For your closing, take prayer requests from the children and use a marker to print them on Band-Aid strips. Attach each Band-Aid strip to a piece of poster paper, vertically and horizontally, gradually building the shape of a cross. Lead the children in a prayer that includes their requests, and conclude by thanking Jesus that He cleans away our sins and makes us well again so that we can live as children of God. Conclude with today's Bible words to remember from Jeremiah 33:3. **God says, "Call to Me and I will answer you."**

18 Jesus Forgives Zacchaeus
Luke 19:1–10

Theme: Jesus changes our hearts.

GATHERING
Set out play money to count and sort. If possible, place the play money in small drawstring bags to tie in with the Bible story illustration. **In today's Bible story we will hear about a man who had lots of money but wasn't happy. He was missing some important things, like friends and, more important, faith in God.**

OPENING
Gather around a table or easel. Draw a large heart on a sheet of paper. Paint the heart red and then paint a blue wash over this, swirling the colors together to make purple. (Practice this in advance. Finger paints work especially well because they are thicker. An alternate method is to mold a red heart from play dough and then knead in lumps of blue play dough to change the color.) Talk about how the two colors totally changed. **Today we will learn about Zacchaeus and how Jesus totally changed his heart and his life by forgiving his sins and bringing him to faith.**

LEARNING
Give each child two pieces of round oat cereal to hold in their hands to represent round coins. Explain that Zacchaeus was a tax collector. People didn't like him because he often took more money than he should and kept it for himself. That was cheating. That was stealing. Demonstrate what Zacchaeus did as you take "coins" (oat cereal) from the children. Say to each child, **You must give me two coins to pay your taxes. One goes to the Roman government.** (And one goes to me!)

Then set out a stepladder on which you have attached several paper leaves. Climb the ladder (tree) as you tell the story about short Zacchaeus climbing a tree to see Jesus. Continue by moving to a table set with several "money bags." Discuss the total change in Zacchaeus. Because of the loving forgiveness of Jesus, Zacchaeus gave back four times to anyone he cheated. (Give each child four pieces of cereal, which can be eaten; do not use the first round of cereal because it was handled by many people.) Zacchaeus also gave half of everything he had to the poor. (Separate the money bags into two piles, one to keep and one to give away.) **The change in Zacchaeus happened because of Jesus. Jesus saves, forgives, and changes us too.**

MOVING
If you have access to a playground, encourage the children to do some climbing on the equipment. Say, **Can you see better up there? That is why Zacchaeus climbed a tree to see Jesus.**

Then have children demonstrate *short* and *tall* through body movements. **Zacchaeus was short; he could not see over the tall people in the crowd.** Have children move to demonstrate other opposites like *large/small, push/pull, stomp/tiptoe,* and so on.

REVIEWING
Gather around a table and have the children imitate your actions as you retell the Bible story. Say, **Many people did not like tax collectors, like Zacchaeus, because they often cheated the people.** *(Reach out as if grabbing money and place it in your pretend pocket.)* **One day, Zacchaeus hurried through the streets because he heard that Jesus was coming to his town, Jericho.** *(Have your right index and middle fingers do the walking, quickly.)* **But Zacchaeus couldn't see anything. The crowd of people was too big and he was too short.** *(Set your left wrist on the table, fingers pointing straight up, to block Zacchaeus—the two fingers on your right hand.)* **But Zacchaeus had a plan. He saw a tree by the road. He climbed the tree and sat on a branch.** *(Place your left elbow on the table, fingers opened wide to represent a tree. Walk the two fingers on your right hand to the "tree," walk them up your left arm, and have your right two fingers sit on a "branch," your left thumb.)* **He not only saw Jesus, Jesus talked to him. Jesus said, "Come down. I will go to your house today." Many people were upset that Jesus would go with such a sinner. They didn't understand. Jesus doesn't like sinful actions.** *(Shake your finger "no.")* **But Jesus loves all people and wants them to repent. Jesus forgave Zacchaeus's sins.** *(Pretend to move something away with a sweep of your arm.)* **And Jesus changed Zacchaeus's heart and life.** *(Cross hands over your heart.)* **Jesus said, "Today salvation has come to this house. . . . For the Son of Man came to seek and to save what was lost" (Luke 19:9–10).** *(Fold your hands.)*

LIVING
Bring out Lucas the Lamb, who says that Zacchaeus is like a lost sheep and Jesus is like the shepherd who saved him. That is what Jesus means when He said He "came to seek and to save what was lost." Say, **You are right, Lucas. All people were lost sinners. But Jesus came to rescue and save us. Jesus not only shows us the way to heaven, He IS the WAY. He takes away our sins and makes us children of God!** Sing about lost sheep in "Sheep Ran Away" *(Lift Little Voices,* p. 46 and on CD).

SINGING
Review the Bible story, singing and using the actions for "Zacchaeus" *(Little Ones Sing Praise,* p. 55). Point out, however, that the most important part of the story is that nothing could keep Jesus away from saving Zacchaeus, not the crowd of people blocking him, not the height of the tree, and not Zacchaeus's sins. Nothing stopped Jesus from finding and rescuing Zacchaeus. Jesus took away his sins and gave him faith and new life. Sing about the love of God in "Nothing Can Keep Us" *(Lift Little Voices,* p. 43 and on CD).

CREATING
Have the children make a picture of Zacchaeus in the tree. Have them place their papers the "tall" way (vertically), draw a tall rectangle for the tree trunk, and color it brown. Then directly above the tree trunk, have each child place his or her hand with fingers open wide, trace around the hand, and color the shape green (to make branches with leaves). A little man can be drawn on the tree. Or make a three-dimensional tree. First, roll a 4 × 6-inch strip of brown paper and tape the edges in place to make a tree trunk. Then take a 4 × 6-inch strip of green paper. Cut slits from one edge to within ½ inch of the other edge to make leafy branches. Tape this to the top of the tree trunk so that the green branches hang down. Draw Zacchaeus on one of the branches. Draw a heart with a cross on the trunk of each tree. Say, **The most important part of the story is the forgiving love of Jesus. He saved us too!**

CLOSING
Explain that God's Word calls us to repent of our sins and change our sinful ways. This happened to Zacchaeus, but this was not something he did. It was the result of Jesus coming to him, calling him to repent, forgiving his sins, and changing his life. Jesus does the same for us today through God's Word and the Sacraments. Read God's words to remember from Mark 1:15: **Repent and believe the good news!** *Option:* Emphasize this change in our hearts with a visual you prepare in advance. (This is slightly complex, but it is worth the effort.) (1) Place a sheet of 8½ × 11-inch paper horizontally. Fold it in half to the right, and then fold it in half to the right again. Reopen it so that there is only one fold, the first fold. (2) Cut a horizontal line from the center point of this fold to the creased line. Make two more similar cuts so that you have four equal sections. Open the page. (3) Now take another sheet of paper and make the same folds. Open the sheet and cut on the creases. Use two of these strips and throw the other two away. (4) Weave the two strips, alternating basket-weave style, through the center slits of the first page. (4) On the middle four sections of the woven strips, draw a white heart with a red outline. (5) Fold the page in half, backward, on the center line. This will open up the woven slips. Separate the woven sections, folding one to the right and the other to the left, revealing a blank woven section. (6) Draw a scribbled black heart on the four middle sections. Now you are ready to demonstrate! Show the scribbled heart to the children, saying this represents sin in each of us. (7) Then pull the underneath, unwoven flaps out to the right and the left, and the hearts will reverse. You will now see the changed, clean heart. Say, **Jesus takes away our sins, cleans our hearts, and changes our lives!**

19 Two Men Pray
Luke 18:9–14

Theme: Pray to the Lord.

GATHERING
Set out real and toy phones that the children can explore and use in role play. Ask, **How do we talk to God?** (In prayer.) **How do we hear what God says to us?** (In the Bible, God's holy Word.)

OPENING
Ask the children, **How many of you like to talk? What do you like to talk about?** Listen to their responses, pointing out some of the similarities to what we talk about in prayer. If some say they like to talk about something they did, you can say, **We can talk to God in prayer about what we do. God likes to listen to us. We can say thank You to God for the special times we have like playing with friends, going on a picnic, or riding to Grandma and Grandpa's house.** If some say they like to talk about things they want, you can say, **God wants to hear about the things we want. You can tell Him that your family wants a new car, or that you want a birthday party, or that you want your uncle to get out of the hospital soon. God listens to what we want. He knows and does what is best for us.** Continue in this manner, pointing out that "asking" is a part of talking to God in prayer, but it is not the only thing. **Let's pray together now: Dear Jesus, thank You for hearing our prayers and answering them in the way You know is best and the time that You know is right. Thank You for taking my sins away and making me a child of God. Amen.**

LEARNING
Say, **God heard our prayer. Now, how can we hear what God has to say to us?** (From the Bible.) Say the words of Jeremiah 31:10: **Hear the word of the Lord!** Then read today's Bible story directly from the Bible after explaining that this is a story Jesus told to teach people about prayer.

Look at the poster picture for this lesson. Point out that this is in the temple-church. The first man, the Pharisee, did not really pray. **God wants us to pray in faith, believing in Him. But the Pharisee wasn't talking to God, he was talking about himself to other people. The Pharisee seemed to be saying, "I'm first. I'm best. You're not." He was bragging about how good he was instead of talking about how good God is. He sounded as if he really didn't need God.**

Point to the tax collector in the poster picture. **The other man prayed according to God's will. He admitted he had sinned and was sorry he had done wrong. He asked for God's mercy. He desperately needed and wanted God's help. And Jesus says that this man, who had faith in the grace of God, went home forgiven.**

So, what have we learned about prayer: (1) prayer is talking to God—this can be with words, in songs, and even just our thoughts because God hears them too; (2) prayers do not have to be long and use fancy, important words—the tax collector's prayer had seven simple words, and Jesus was pleased because he said it in faith, trusting in God; (3) our prayers are about God's will for our lives—not just about what we want—because God knows what is best for us.

MOVING
Have the children stand in a circle and toss a Koosh ball back and forth to each other. Each time a child catches the Koosh ball, the child is to identify a *time* when we can pray to God (such as morning, noon, bedtime, mealtime, playtime). **We can pray to God any time! God is always ready to hear our prayers and answer them.**

Have the children stand in two lines that face each other. Show them how to bounce-pass a large playground ball (throwing it to the ground so it bounces up to a team member in the other line). The child who catches the ball is to identify a *place* where we can pray to God (such as in the car, in your own room, at the beach). **We can pray to God anywhere! He is always near and can hear our thoughts and words.**

REVIEWING
Rather than review the Bible story, use this time to review types of prayers. Give the children a theme, listen to and write down their prayer requests, then pray together (either repeating their requests or letting volunteers do so). Possibilities follow:

1. Identify the five senses. Thank God for what you see (pretty flowers, tall mountains), what you hear (bird songs, ocean waves), what you touch (velvety soft ducks, slimy mud), what you smell (Mom's perfume, cookies baking), and what you taste (cheeseburgers, chocolate).

2. Name colors and have children identify things of that color for which we give thanks.

3. Draw a sad face and a happy face. Identify situations that are happy and sad. Ask God to help us in sad times, and thank Him for the blessings of happy times.

4. Have children name plants and then name animals. Praise God for creating them, and thank Him for blessing our lives through them.

5. Consider other topics and themes related to your blessings and needs (such as types of weather, articles of clothing).

LIVING
Bring out Lucas the Lamb, who tells the children something else about prayer. Lucas demonstrates various prayer postures and the children can imitate him. People pray standing, sitting, kneeling, and even bowed down. People may fold their hands, have palms touching each other, cross their arms over their hearts, or raise them high. **The position you are in can remind you to be quietly humble, to give glory to God, or to focus your thoughts only on your prayer. But to God, what is most important is what is in your heart. God looks for faith in our hearts, faith that believes in Jesus as our Savior and trusts the promises of God.**

SINGING
Read the thank-You prayer on page 34 of *Lift Little Voices*. Then say, **Sometimes we sing our prayers instead of speak them. Let's sing this thank-You prayer.** (Music is available on the CD.) *Option:* Several songs that can teach us more about prayer are found on pages 14 and 15 of *Little Ones Sing Praise* (available from CPH). These songs include "God, Our Father, Hear Your Children," "I Am Sorry, Jesus," "Jesus Listens When I Pray," and "We Pray for Each Other."

CREATING
Let children make their own "Thank-You Prayer Books." Provide each child with at least four envelopes. (Bright colored envelopes from an office-supply store give an interesting look). Either draw or glue a picture of a prayer theme on each envelope. Children may cut out pictures from catalogues and magazines that are related to the themes. (Themes: clothing, toys, household items, food.) Children are to place their pictures in the related envelopes. When finished, stack each person's envelopes and staple them together on the left side to make a booklet. Use one child's booklet, taking out and displaying the pictures as you say prayers of thanks for the items.

For another prayer project, give each child a plain paper lunch bag to decorate with marking pens, glitter pens, and stickers. Have children take the bags home and use them to gather items representing things for which they are thankful (such as a picture of their families, their pet's toy). Include these in your prayer time if any children return these bags in weeks to come.

CLOSING
Give each child a removable Post-it note to place on something in the room that can be included in an asking or thanking prayer. From an open Bible read today's words to remember from Psalm 86:6: **Hear my prayer, O Lord.** Have the children repeat these words after each (creative) prayer petition that you say, as you go around the room collecting the Post-it notes.

20 The Good Samaritan
Luke 10:30–36

Theme: Share God's love with all people.

GATHERING
Set out a big lump of play dough in the middle of the table. Tell the children they can look at it. Pause, and then comment, **Looking at this doesn't do much good, does it? I think we want to get our hands on it and do something with it!** Let the children play with the play dough as you say, **In today's Bible story we will hear about two people who just looked when something needed to be done. Then we will hear about a man we call the Good Samaritan. When he looked, he got his hands on the problem right away and did something about it!**

OPENING
Have the children sit in a circle. Say, **Your neighbor is the person right next to you.** Ask them to shake hands with their neighbor on both sides. **In today's Bible story, Jesus tells us that our neighbor is anyone who needs our help and care. Our neighbor can be someone close by or someone far away.** Together make a neighbor/friend web. Take a ball of yarn, wrap the end of the yarn around your wrist several times and then toss the ball to someone across the circle. Have the children continue the procedure. When you have a web interconnecting many people, say, **This friendship web reminds us that our neighbors and friends can be people near us or people farther away. Let's listen to a Bible story that Jesus told about neighbors and friends.**

LEARNING
Read the story directly from the Bible. Luke 10:30–36 is brief but packed with action. After reading the story, have the children act it out. Start *after* the robbers have attacked. Spread a few trickles of ketchup (blood) on the arms and face of the person playing the injured man. Instruct the "priest and Levite" to look but not come near the injured man. Then have the Samaritan go directly to the man, wipe off his "wounds" with a cloth, help him up, and take him to a place (chair) where he can be helped. Say, **One of the amazing things about the Good Samaritan is that he came from another country. He was not a nearby neighbor like the priest and Levite. In fact, many people in Israel considered Samaritans to be "no-good enemies."** But this did not stop him. He saw someone who needed help, so he got busy. He did more than clean the man's wounds. In fact, he took the man to a hotel to rest and stayed up all night watching to see if the man needed more help. In fact, he gave the hotel owner two silver coins to pay the hotel bill. In fact, he said he would pay for any extra bills that came along. He went way out of his way to help someone else. This makes me think of Jesus. Jesus went way out of His way to help you and me. In fact, Jesus came all the way from heaven and lived on earth in order to help us. In fact, He completely paid for our sins by dying on the cross and arising at Easter. Now Jesus leads us to be His people. He takes away our sins and guides and empowers us to show His love to others. Jesus leads us to be friends and neighbors to people close by and to those far away. Jesus loves all people and wants us to love others too.**

MOVING
Have races with pairs of partners. In one race, partners hold hands as they run; another race, partners run back-to-back; another race, partners run with their foreheads touching each other. Children will need to work together to be successful.

Let children have free time exploring the use of hula hoops. Then play a game where the children spin their hoops on the floor and do a directed action until the hoop stops spinning. When the hoop stops, the child should sit down on the floor and rest. Possible directed actions are: run in place, jump, twirl around, skip, and so on.

REVIEWING
Have the children clap along with you on the following rhythmic (not rhyming) narration. Each line has a count of 3 or 4 claps. On the third line of each stanza (marked with an *) give many rushed claps, except for the third line of the last stanza, which should be done slowly.

There was a man from Jerusalem
Who traveled through the land.
*A group of robbers knocked him down
And took all that he had.

The poor man waited for someone to help.
A priest! Now would he stop?
*No, he was too busy or afraid
And hurried on his way.

Oh, aches and pains, he needed help soon.
A Levite surely would stop.
*But, no! The Levite rushed on his way,
Ignoring the injured man's cries.

Now look, here comes a Samaritan.
They were not friends, that's for sure.
He stopped . . . he helped . . . he rescued . . . he stayed
To give the man help that day.

LIVING
Bring out Lucas the Lamb, who says that the Good Samaritan reminds him of the Good Shepherd, who reminds him of Jesus. Say, **Yes, Jesus is the one who is truly good. We aren't; we are sinners. But Jesus forgives our sins. And then He changes our hearts and lives so that we can learn from Him and His Word. Jesus leads us to live for Him, showing goodness and kindness to others. Jesus said, "As I have loved you . . . love one another" (John 13:34).**

SINGING
Sing "The Good Shepherd" (*Lift Little Voices*, p. 25 and on CD). Also sing "We Love" and "Love, Love, Love" (*Little Ones Sing Praise*, pp. 54 and 30), emphasizing that any love and kindness we share has its beginnings in the transforming power of God Himself.

CREATING
Fittingly, the two suggested projects will need people working together, helping each other. Say, **We've talked a lot about neighbors today. Let's make a map or picture of a neighborhood.** Place a large sheet of mural paper on the floor or a table. Draw streets for the neighborhood. Let children use blocks to build the homes and other buildings. They can also draw in things like trees, swing sets, stops signs, and so on. Perhaps let them place toy cars on the streets too.

Then make a "helping hands" wreath. Have children trace around their hands on various shades of brown paper, from light to darker, and cut out the shapes. Arrange the hands on a wreath shape cut from poster paper (cut out a circle within a circle). Say, **We use our helping hands to show loving-kindness to others because God, first of all, showed love to us. He changed our hearts and lives by forgiving us through Jesus and making us His own people.** To represent this, have the children draw a heart with a cross shape on each of the hands.

CLOSING
Cut out red hearts on which you have drawn a cross (similar to the design on the "helping hands" wreath). Use rolls of tape to attach these hearts to the top of both hands of all the children in your group. Say, **Jesus is our Good Samaritan, Good Shepherd, Good Savior. He changes our hearts and lives, forgiving our sins, and leading us to follow His ways and to live as children of God.** Read today's Bible words to remember from John 13:34: **Jesus said, "As I have loved you . . . love one another."** Discuss ways the children can share this love with family, friends, and neighbors everywhere. Then pray for God's guidance.

21 Jairus's Daughter
Luke 8:40–56

Theme: Jesus is true God.

GATHERING
In shoebox lids, place similar items that children can arrange from smallest to biggest. (Sets might include pencils, fun foam shapes, leaves, or toy cars, all of different sizes.) As the children work say, **Sometimes we have small problems. Sometimes we have bigger problems. Today we will hear a Bible story about the man Jairus who had a very, very big problem. So he went to Jesus for help.**

OPENING
Hold up a cell phone and say, **If I want to talk to someone far away, I can punch in their number on my cell phone;** hold up a car key and pretend to turn it in the ignition and say, **If I want to start my car, I turn the key. But God doesn't need anything like a phone or a key or any kind of tool when He wants to do something. God just says the word and it happens. Remember when God made the world? He said, "Let there be light," and there was light. Remember when Jesus was in a boat on a lake during a storm? Jesus just said, "Peace! Be still." And the storm stopped. Today we will hear again about the great power of Jesus. With just a word He brought someone who was dead back to life. How could Jesus do that? Jesus is true God; He is almighty!**

LEARNING
In advance, prepare a puppet of Jairus's daughter from a brown paper lunch bag. Lay the bag flat and draw closed eyes and her hair on the flap and draw a smile below the flap. Then lift up the flap and draw her hair again and her eyes opened. Tell the Bible story, emphasizing that the father went to Jesus and prayed for help. When you tell that the daughter died, show the puppet with the eyes closed (flap down) and hold the puppet flat in your lap. When you talk about Jesus telling her to get up, hold the puppet up, pushing the flap up too so that her open eyes can be seen. Ask, **How was Jesus able to do this?** (Because He is true God; He is almighty!) Call attention to the happy scene on the poster picture. The little girl was alive and well and ready to eat!

Continue with three more paper bags. Say, **Jesus saves us by taking care of our three biggest problems.** Identify these three problems as *sin, death,* and *the power of the devil.* Draw ugly, squiggly lines on the three bags as you identify these words. **Jesus took our sins** (blow up one of the bags and pop it) **when He died on the cross so that we are now forgiven. And Jesus conquered death** (blow up another bag and pop it) **when He came to life again at Easter. So Jesus has power over the devil** (blow up and pop the third bag), **and He promises us eternal life with Him in heaven. Jesus has won the victory! Hooray! Jesus is true God! He is almighty!**

MOVING
Take a break and run some races where everyone is a winner. The first race can be done with one or more lines of runners. The goal is to run through the finish line, which is an open newspaper page held on each side by helpers. The children will break through the paper like runners breaking through the tape at the finish line. Be sure that the helpers also get a chance to run. (Children do not need to race against each other; they just race to break the finish line.)

Have an obstacle race. Set out four or more large boxes (at least two-feet square). Tape a large number on one or more sides of each box. Set them randomly in your play area. Children are to run around each box in consecutive order. (Children may follow directly behind you or other children if they seem unsure about the numbers.) Mix up the boxes and try it again

REVIEWING
Sing the following stanzas to the melody of "Jesus Loves Me, This I Know." Children can echo each phrase that you sing and join in singing the refrain.

1. Once a leader came to say,
   "Jesus, help my girl today.
   She is dying. Only You
   Have the power to rescue."

   (Refrain)
   Jesus is true God. Jesus is true God.
   Jesus is true God. He saves from sin and death.

2. But the little girl died
   And the people cried and cried.
   Jesus said, "My child, get up."
   Just like that the girl stood up. *(Refrain)*

3. Jesus has the power to save
   Us from Satan, sin, and grave.
   He removes our sin and strife
   And He gives eternal life. *(Refrain)*

LIVING
Bring out Lucas the Lamb, who says, **That was a happy Bible story. But I know a story that is not so happy. My people-friend Brian is sad. His grandmother died in the hospital. Will Jesus make her alive again?** Answer that Jesus will, but in a different way. Jesus promised that on the very last day of the world He will return and bring all believers in Him to live eternally with Him in heaven. **Listen to what the Bible tells us about heaven. Job 19:25–27 says, "I know that my Redeemer lives, and that in the end He will stand upon the earth. . . . I will see God; I myself will see Him with my own eyes." 1 John 3:2 says, "We know that when He appears, we shall be like him, for we shall see him as He is." Our life in heaven will be perfect. Revelation 21:4 says, "There will be no more death or mourning or crying or pain." And Psalm 16:11 says, "You will fill me with joy in Your presence, with eternal pleasures at Your right hand."** Have Lucas the Lamb say, **So someday Brian will see his grandmother in heaven. So his story has a happy ending after all!**

SINGING
Say, **We can be sure that we and all believers in Jesus will go to heaven. Listen to the words of Jesus in the Bible (John 10:28): "I give them eternal life, and . . . no one can snatch them out of My hand."** This concept is reinforced in the words of the song "Nothing Can Keep Us" (*Lift Little Voices*, p. 43 and on CD). Also sing "God So Loved the World," which tells us the saving faith we have in God's plan of salvation (*Lift Little Voices*, p. 33 and on CD).

CREATING
The father in the Bible story, Jairus, prayed that Jesus would help him. Make necklaces that remind us to pray. Explain first that some people pray with their hands touching their opposite shoulder, crossing their arms over their heart. A looped pretzel represents the crossed arms, and is a reminder to pray. Give each child in your group at least eight looped pretzels. Let the children weave a length of yarn through the pretzels to make a necklace that can be tied at the neck. (Hint: First wrap one end of the yarn in tape to make it sturdy for weaving.) Suggest that the children explain the prayer pretzels to their parents and then place the necklaces on a tree or shrub branch to feed the birds or squirrels.

Children can also make a bracelet with a message. Cut the cardboard tube from a roll of paper towels into one-inch widths to make individual bracelets. Slit through the back of the bracelet so it is easy to manage. Let children wrap the bracelet in aluminum foil. Then give each child three dot stickers to place across the top of the bracelet. Children may use thin-point markers to draw a symbol on each sticker—the letter *I*, a heart, a cross. This message says: *I love Jesus.*

CLOSING
Hold up a large gray cloud shape and behind it hold the shape of a yellow sun. Say, **Even on a gloomy cloudy day, we know** (place the sun in front of the cloud) **that the sun is there. And in our lives, even when we have problems and troubles, we know that God is there. He is with us, He does what is best for us, He forgives us for Jesus' sake, and He promises eternal life in heaven!** From the Bible read today's words to remember from Isaiah 6:3: **Holy, holy, holy is the Lord Almighty.**

22 The Lord's Supper
Matthew 26:17–30

Theme: Jesus gave Himself for us.

GATHERING
In advance prepare brown sheets of paper on which you have attached white half-dollar-size circles, varying in number from 1–10. Print the corresponding number on each paper. Ask the appropriate church leader if you can borrow the church's individual Communion cups. When children arrive, they are to match the cups with the circular wafer shapes. See if any of the children know where the little cups are used. Discuss that in church services, at the Lord's Supper, people receive flatbread and then wine in either small cups or a large chalice. **Today we will learn more about the day Jesus first gave the Lord's Supper and why our church continues to celebrate that special meal.**

OPENING
Point out that many celebrations have food connected to them. Hold up a candy cane and ask, **With what celebration do we eat candy canes?** (Christmas) Hold up a cupcake and ask when we always have cake. (At a birthday celebration) Ask, **What food do we usually eat when we celebrate the Fourth of July?** (Hot dogs and hamburgers) **At which celebration do we eat turkey and pumpkin pie?** (Thanksgiving) Continue, **In our Bible story today, Jesus and His disciples were going to eat a meal to celebrate the Passover. They were celebrating the time when God used Moses to lead the people of Israel out of slavery in Egypt. Each year at the Passover meal the people ate roasted lamb, salad with bitter dressing, flat bread, and wine. After eating the Passover meal, Jesus stood up and said He would give them a new meal, a new supper, to celebrate. He gave what we call the Lord's Supper. Let's learn more about it.**

LEARNING
(Note: For many children, this may be their introduction to the Lord's Supper. Approach the discussion with wonder, awe, and mystery because, though we may try to explain, we cannot understand the mysteries of almighty God. Children, probably more than most people, accept this on the basis of trust. Do *not* act out the Lord's Supper, giving the children food. This will confuse them and lead them to think they have received the Lord's Supper.)

Explain that though the Passover meal was a happy celebration, Jesus seemed sad. He knew that the next day He would suffer and die to take away the sins of the world. Jesus had told His disciples that this would happen, but they still didn't seem to understand. Just like you and me, the disciples were weak and sinful. So Jesus gave His special meal. Take some flatbread (pita bread) and tear it into pieces and say, **The Bible tells us that Jesus took bread and broke it and gave it to His disciples saying, "Take and eat; this is My body."** Then hold up a silver chalice from your church or one that you have made (see the "Creating" section). **The Bible tells us that Jesus then gave thanks and said, "Drink from it all of you. This is the new covenant (promise) in My blood." Jesus said to do this often to remember Him. He gave this gift with the promised blessings of forgiveness, life, and salvation.**

Tell the children that, just as Jesus told us to do, the church continues to regularly offer the Lord's Supper. Someday when the children are older and have received special instruction, they too will be able to take the Lord's Supper. Remind them that they already have the gifts of forgiveness, life, and salvation through God's Word and Baptism. God loves us so much He pours out His grace and promises in many ways!

MOVING
Practice *go*, *freeze*, and *melt* commands. When you say *go*, child are to do the action you have suggested. (Possibilities: run in place, hop on one foot, jump, wave arms). When you say *freeze*, children should stop and hold their position very still. When you say *melt*, the children should "slither" down to the floor as if melting and curl up as if lying in a puddle. Repeat this procedure several times. For another activity, give the children colorful scarves and ribbons to wave as they move their bodies in time and with the flow of recorded classical music.

REVIEWING
Ask your pastor to describe the procedures that take place in the Lord's Supper, to speak the words he uses at the Lord's Supper, and to talk about the supper's blessings. Perhaps he can come to your room, or if possible, he can meet you in the church sanctuary. If the pastor is unable to come, perhaps you can show a video recording of the Lord's Supper taken during a church worship service.

LIVING
Bring out Lucas the Lamb to ask some questions. He says, **I still don't understand. In the Lord's Supper, do the people receive bread and wine or do they get Jesus' body and blood?** Say, **We receive all of that and more! In the Lord's Supper, all at the same time, Jesus offers us bread and wine, His body and blood, *and* forgiveness, life, and salvation! All of that is there *in, with, and under* the bread and wine.** Lucas adds that it is still a mystery to him. Respond, **Yes, it is a mystery. And it is a miracle. It happens because it is a gift from our almighty God!** Lucas asks how God does this mystery and miracle. You respond, **This happens by the Word of God, which is almighty and powerful. Remember, we talked about how God created the world by saying the words "Let it be." And Jesus said the words "Peace, be still," and the storm stopped. And Jesus said the words "Get up," and the dead girl became alive. It is the Word of God that gives the body and blood of Jesus and forgiveness, life, and salvation along with the bread and wine in the Lord's Supper!** Lucas the Lamb then responds, **Now it makes sense to me! It is through the powerful Word of God. If Jesus says it, I know it is true!**

SINGING
Ask, **If Jesus knew that the next day He would die on the cross, why didn't He try to escape and leave town?** (Jesus loved us so much, He was willing to suffer and die for us.) Sing "God So Loved the World" (*Lift Little Voices*, p. 33 and on CD). *Option:* Consider using the book *Journey to Easter* in this and the next few lessons. The book, available from Concordia Publishing House, has beautiful pictures of the events of Holy Week, and it takes children through the week, counting off from 1–10. Numbers 1 and 2 would especially apply to this lesson. If you do review the Palm Sunday event leading up to today's story, you may want to listen to the song "March On, Little Donkey" (*Lift Little Voices*, p. 26 and on CD).

CREATING
Have the children make "silver chalices" as a reminder of the cup that was used at the Lord's Supper. (Note that the chalice is the item missing on the student page.) Give each child a plastic stemmed glass (a plastic wine glass, available in quantities at party stores). Provide sheets of aluminum foil to wrap around the cups and mold into place. Add more foil if there are bare spots. Mention that as the children press the foil into place, it will wrinkle, which is good because the wrinkles catch the light and make the cup sparkle more. **This cup reminds us of that evening Jesus gave the Lord's Supper.**

Remember that Jesus did all things because He loves the people of the world. Have children make "people" shapes to represent themselves. Use a rectangular cracker for the body, a round cracker for the head, and stick pretzels for arms and legs. Attach the pieces with cheese that squirts from a can. Then "clothe" the person shape with cheese. If possible, add a red candy heart to the person shape as a reminder of the love of Jesus in our hearts. (If you prefer to use cookie shapes for the body and head, use frosting from a tube instead of cheese.)

CLOSING
Point out that the Lord's Supper is also called Communion, the Lord's Table, or the Feast of the Eucharist (which is a way of saying the Meal of Thanksgiving). Sing the refrain "This is the *feast of victory* for our God. Alleluia, alleluia, alleluia." (See *Little Ones Sing Praise*, p. 95 or a Lutheran hymnal.) The *victory* is that Jesus has saved us by His death and resurrection. From an open Bible, read today's words to remember from 1 Timothy 1:15: **Christ Jesus came into the world to save sinners.**

23 Jesus on Trial
John 18:28–19:16

Theme: Jesus leads us to forgive.

GATHERING
Prepare puzzle packs for the children. Cut out heart shapes of different colors and draw a cross on each one with a black marker. Cut each heart into two puzzle pieces. Mix them up and place them in a ziplock plastic bag. Make several of these puzzle packs for the children to work on. Say, **These hearts make me think of a special message we have in the Bible:** *Jesus loves and forgives us, and He leads us to love and forgive others.* **These are the two parts of a happy heart.**

OPENING
In advance, prepare two paper crowns that are topped with many pointed triangular shapes. (These can be headband style with the ends taped together to fit.) One crown should be yellow (gold), and perhaps you can add glitter to make it sparkle. The other should be from gray paper and with no glitter. Put on the gold crown and ask who might wear a crown. **A king or queen is an important person. They often wear a gold crown and are very rich. Today we will hear about a different kind of crown. This was a crown that the enemies of Jesus made for Him to hurt Him and to laugh at Him and to ridicule Him. It was a crown of thorns.** Take the gray crown, turn it so the points are pointing down, and use a black marker to draw X-shaped thorns around the band and on the points of the crown. **This was a sad and hurtful crown that Jesus wore when He suffered for the sins of the world, for you and me. Let's learn more about what happened.**

LEARNING
Explain that after Jesus had given the Lord's Supper to His disciples, they went to the Garden of Gethsemane to pray. There Jesus' enemies captured Him, made Him their prisoner, and put Him on trial. Jesus could have escaped because He has all power; He is true God. But Jesus willingly let Himself be taken away, knowing He would suffer and die on the cross, because He wanted to save us from sin and its punishment. Jesus was put on trial before Annas and Caiaphas. But the enemies needed the verdict of the Roman governor, Pontius Pilate, in order to put Jesus to death. Explain the trial with Pilate, using a wooden gavel (or hammer) and this three-part pattern.

First, Pilate talked to Jesus and asked Him questions. (Bang the gavel.) Pilate said, "This man is not guilty!" But the enemies shouted, "Crucify Him." Then Pilate got an idea! He sent Jesus to King Herod. But that didn't work. King Herod sent Jesus back to Pilate. So . . .

Second, Pilate talked to Jesus and asked Him questions. (Bang the gavel.) Pilate said, "This man is not guilty!" But the enemies shouted, "Crucify Him." Then Pilate got an idea! He would give the people a choice: set Jesus free or set Barabbas, a murderer, free. But that didn't work. The people shouted, "Give us Barrabbas. So . . .

Third, Pilate talked to Jesus and asked Him questions. (Bang the gavel.) Pilate said, "This man is not guilty!" But the enemies shouted, "Crucify Him." Then Pilate got an idea! He had Jesus beaten with whips and a crown of thorns placed on His head. Then people would feel sorry for Him. But that didn't work. The enemies still shouted, "Crucify Him." So Pilate said, "Okay. Take Him away."

Jesus had done nothing wrong. He was not guilty. But He was punished—for us! Let's pray: Dear Jesus, thank You for taking away our sins. Help us to be forgiving of others, just as You have forgiven us. Amen.

MOVING
Make bowling pins by filling empty plastic liter soda bottles about ⅓ full of sand. Reseal the bottles and line them up. Let children roll a playground ball at the pins to see how many they can knock over. Place the pins at a higher level, such as on a stair step or ledge. Children will have to throw the ball through the air to knock pins over.

REVIEWING
(Note: If you are using the book *Journey to Easter* to tell about Holy Week, numbers 3 and 4 would apply to this lesson.) To reinforce the main concept of this Bible story, you will need the gavel again, red Post-it notes, a black marker, and a large cross, either a standing cross or one drawn on paper.

Say, **Jesus was not guilty. But we are. Think in your heart: Have you ever been selfish?** Bang the gavel and say, **We are guilty!** In a prominent manner, mark a large check mark on a red Post-it note, and place the note on the cross.

Continue this pattern with other questions, asking **Have you ever said something that was not true? Have you ever lost your temper? Have you ever hurt someone? Have you ever said unkind words? Have you ever disobeyed your mom or dad? Have you ever cheated in a game?**

Then say, **We are all guilty of doing wrong things. All people are sinners. We are guilty.** (Pound the gavel and wave a red note.) **But look what we just did. We gave our guilt to Jesus. He took the punishment for our sins when He died on the cross. Why did Jesus do that?** (He loves us so much.) **This is a sad story and a happy story. It is sad that Jesus suffered, but we are happy that He saved us!**

LIVING
Distribute the children's pages, compare them to the poster picture, and see what is missing. (Jesus' crown of thorns) Have children draw lines or Xs to make the thorns. Then bring out Lucas the Lamb, who says, **Teacher, Teacher, I remember another Bible story that had thorns in it.** Have Lucas flip through the poster pictures till he finds the picture of Adam and Eve after the fall into sin. Say, **Good thinking, Lucas. Not only do both pictures show thorns, the pictures are connected by sin and a Savior. When Adam and Eve first sinned, God promised them a Savior, and that Savior was Jesus, who came to take away the sins of the whole world. God loves us and keeps His promises. Because of Jesus, we can be certain that He will keep His promise to take us and all believers in Jesus to heaven!**

SINGING
The message of Jesus our Savior is an important message to share with other people. Just like Jesus leads us to share forgiveness with other people, He also wants us to share the Good News of salvation. Sing about that in "You've Got to Tell" (*Lift Little Voices*, p. 42 and on CD) and also in "Go Tell" (*Little Ones Sing Praise*, p. 104).

CREATING
Provide large poster paper heart shapes that the children can trace around, using a black crayon or marker on red paper. Then have children draw Xs on the heart outline as a reminder of the crown of thorns. **Jesus loved us so much, He was willing to suffer a crown of thorns and death on a cross.** On each heart print a message with each child's name, saying "Jesus loves (name)." Let children write their own names if they are able.

Say again that this is a sad, yet happy story. **It is sad that Jesus was sent to die on a cross. But we can be happy too, because Jesus saved us when He died.** Make a cross (sad) that is beautiful (happy). Give each child a wide cross that is drawn on poster paper. You will need to precut the crosses unless the children are able to do this themselves. Let children glue dry, uncooked pasta to the cross shapes for texture and decoration. Then have the children paint the crosses with gold paint. (Note: You may want to punch a hole near the top of each cross before adding the pasta so the cross can be hung from a nail.)

CLOSING
In advance, prepare a plastic photo cube with pictures you have cut from a magazine, drawn yourself, or photographed. Pictures are to give suggestions of things for which we can be thankful. One of the pictures should show a cross, and the others might include food, clothing, a house, toys, family, and so on. Sit in a circle and let each child have the opportunity to gently roll the cube to see what you will give thanks for in prayer. (You can expect some repetition.) When the cross appears, say, **We have many things for which we can be thankful. But above all, we thank God for Jesus who takes away our sins and promises us eternal life in heaven.** Close with today's words to remember from Colossians 3:13: **Forgive as the Lord forgave you.**

24 Jesus on the Cross   John 19:17–37

Theme: Jesus died to save us.

GATHERING

Have the children use rolling pins to roll out a sheet of play dough. From this, they can make crosses using cross-shaped cookie cutters. Or they can use plastic knives to trim out a large square and from this, cut smaller squares out of each corner to make a cross shape. Say, **Jesus died on the cross to take away our sins.**

OPENING

Display several decorative crosses and cross jewelry that are shiny and pretty. Say, **These crosses are beautiful. We show them to honor Jesus and give Him the glory. But the cross Jesus suffered on was not pretty. It was rough and ugly and caused a lot of pain. As sad as the cross is, we can also be happy as we look to Easter when, just as Jesus said He would, He arose from the dead on the third day. Jesus is true God with almighty power. Let's learn more about what happened.**

LEARNING

Display today's poster picture. Also have available a rope, purple fabric, a rough piece of wood, large nails, a natural sponge, white strips of fabric, and a rock, each placed in separate brown paper lunch bags. (Note: Keep these items available for the next session, as a review.)

Remind the children that Jesus had been captured by His enemies. **At the trial with the Roman governor, Pontius Pilate declared that Jesus was not guilty. But still Pilate had Jesus whipped.** (Set out the rope.) **The soldiers mocked Jesus, saying He was a king with no power. They put a crown of thorns on His head and had Him wear a purple robe.** (Set out the purple fabric.) **Then Pilate turned Jesus over to His enemies to be crucified.** (Display the rough wood and the nails.) Note that the cross was like rough, unpolished wood from a tree; that is why we often say Jesus was nailed to a tree. **When Jesus was thirsty, they gave Him something to drink from a sponge.** (Set out the sponge.) **They didn't give Him water, they gave Him smelly, bitter vinegar! While Jesus was on the cross, the sky got as dark as night for three hours. This showed God's sorrow at what was happening. When Jesus died, He said, "It is finished." He had done everything that was needed to save us and take away our sins. A spear was pushed into Jesus' side to make sure He was dead. A Roman centurion, captain of the guards, watched and said, "Truly He is the Son of God." Friends of Jesus took His lifeless body from the cross and wrapped it in long white strips of cloth for burial.** (Set out white fabric.) **Jesus was placed in a grave that was like a cave carved out of a hillside. A large stone was placed at the entrance to close the tomb.** (Set out the rock.) **This was a sad day. Our church colors on this day are black to honor Jesus. But this is not the end of the story. Jesus died, as He said He would, and on the third day He came alive again, just as He said.** Distribute the children's page. Point out that the cross is empty because Jesus died and was buried. But we also know that on the third day, His tomb was empty because Jesus arose from the dead at Easter.

MOVING

This is a very important and serious lesson, but children need a little break, with time to release energy and tension. Play a wiggle game in which you give instructions to wiggle different parts of their body. Tell them you will use the soldier's command "halt" when each movement is to end. Then play a game with hula hoops that are placed on the ground. Say that each hula hoop is a tree, they are squirrels, and each tree can only hold one squirrel. You or a volunteer will chase and try to tag the squirrels who are running loose and are not safe in a tree. But if a running squirrel jumps into a hoop (tree), the safe squirrel has to leave and run away. When a squirrel is tagged, that squirrel becomes the one who chases after the other squirrels.

REVIEWING

(Note: If you are referring to the book *Journey to Easter* from CPH, numbers 5, 6, and 7 pertain to this lesson.) Use this time to add more details about Jesus on the cross. Say, **Jesus spoke seven times from the cross. The first three times He was thinking about the needs of other people. He forgave the people who were hurting him, He promised heaven to the believing thief next to Him, and He asked His disciple John to take care of His mother, Mary. Jesus said:**

1. Father, forgive them, for they do not know what they are doing.
2. I tell you the truth, today you will be with Me in Paradise.
3. Dear woman, here is your son. Here is your mother.

   Then Jesus spoke twice about His great suffering.

4. My God, My God, why have You forsaken Me?
5. I am thirsty.

   Then Jesus knew He had done everything for our salvation and He was ready to die. This is what He said.

6. It is finished.
7. Father, into Your hands I commit My spirit.

LIVING

Bring out Lucas the Lamb, who is wearing a little, colorful neck scarf and seems very happy. He explains that his family made him happy by trading things with him. First, his sister saw his old, dirty, ragged neck scarf, and she said, **Let's trade. I'll take yours and you can have my new, colorful scarf.** Then when the family stopped for fast food, he sadly looked under the bun lid and saw just a plain, dry hamburger. His mother said, **Let's trade. I'll take yours and you can have my cheeseburger with ketchup.** Then the family was going bike riding, but Lucas had a flat tire. His dad said, **Let's trade. I'll take your bike and fix it while you take my bike and go riding with the others. Why did they all make trades that were good for Lucas but not so good for them?** (Because they love him.) Then emphasize that in a much bigger and more important way, that is what Jesus did for us. It was as if Jesus said to us, **Let's trade. I'll take your sins to the cross and you can have my holiness and righteousness so that you can live in heaven someday. Why did Jesus make that great trade? Because He loves us!**

SINGING

Since we don't want to sing about an unfinished story, the song suggested for today includes both Jesus' death and resurrection. Sing "Glory, Glory, Lord Jesus" (*Lift Little Voices*, p. 27 and on CD). *Option:* From *Little Ones Sing Praise*, pages 92 and 93 sing "Jesus Came from Heaven," "Glory Be to Jesus," and "Do You Know Who Died for Me."

CREATING

Make a stained-glass picture. Children are to tear shapes from a variety of colors of tissue paper and glue these onto a sheet of white paper. When the page is covered with colored paper, have the children trace over the edge of each shape with a black marking pen. Provide patterns so children can trace and cut out a cross from black paper (or precut black crosses for the children) and glue these on the center of the colored page. (This takes an idea from an earlier lesson and develops it two steps further.)

Make another cross that looks forward to Easter. Have children glue a large and small wooden craft stick together to make a cross. Insert the cross into a lump of play dough that represents the hill on which Jesus' cross was placed (Calvary/Golgotha). Have children press tiny silk flowers (from a craft store) into the play dough hill to decorate it.

CLOSING

Place masking tape on the floor in the shape of a large cross. Have the children sit on the tape so that they form a cross shape too. Teach them how to make the sign of the cross on themselves (head to chest, shoulder to shoulder). Read John 3:16 and say a prayer thanking Jesus for saving us from sin, death, and the devil. Then say together today's Bible words to remember from 1 Corinthians 15:3: **Christ died for our sins.**

25 Jesus Greets Mary Magdalene at Easter *John 20:1–18*

Theme: Jesus is alive.

GATHERING
Hide pictures of Jesus around the room. When children arrive, set them on a search for the pictures. Point out, **In today's Bible story we will see that no one had to go looking for Jesus, because He came to them! Jesus comes to us today in His holy Word in the Bible and also in the Sacraments of Baptism and the Lord's Supper.**

OPENING
Set out the seven bags of items related to last session's Bible story plus one more. Use them to briefly review what happened on Good Friday. Then say, **Oh, look! We have an extra bag. Let's look inside to see what is there.** Open the eighth bag, which is empty, and let each child have a look inside. Then say, **What a surprise! The bag is empty! On Easter Sunday, it was an even bigger surprise when people came to Jesus' tomb and found that it was empty! Angels told them, "I know that you are looking for Jesus, who was crucified. He is not here; He has risen, just as He said" (Matthew 28:5–6). Let's learn more about that happy day.**

LEARNING
Prepare two scenes in advance, either on a chalkboard or mural paper. Display a scene on one side of the room showing several crowded-together, square Bible-times houses with rectangular windows and doors. This will represent the city of Jerusalem. On the other side of the room display a picture of the open tomb—draw a hillside with a round opening and a round stone next to it, and perhaps add a few simple trees and flowers. As you tell the Easter story, start by walking away from the picture of Jerusalem, explaining that on Easter Sunday, early in the morning, three women went to the tomb to put perfumes and oils on the dead body of Jesus (much like today, people send flowers to a funeral). Stop before you get to the tomb picture and say that the women saw the stone had been rolled away. Run back to "Jerusalem" saying that Mary Magdalene ran back to town to tell Peter and John that the stone had been rolled away. Then walk to the tomb and say that in the meantime the other two women went to the tomb to have a closer look. Tell what the angels said, then run to the middle of the room and stop because Jesus stopped the women on their way back to town. After talking to Jesus, they ran on to Jerusalem, excited to tell others that Jesus had arisen. Then run back to the tomb saying that next Peter and John ran to see what had happened. Then walk back and return again to indicate that they walked back to Jerusalem, and Mary Magdalene returned to the tomb. Tell her part of the story from John 20, referring also to the poster picture in the Teachers Guide and number 8 in the book *Journey to Easter*. Conclude with Mary running back to Jerusalem to tell everyone she had seen Jesus. **This was just the beginning of the day. We'll see that there was much more to happen!**

MOVING
Comment on all the running back and forth that the people did that first Easter Sunday. They were so excited. They wanted to tell everyone the Good News that Jesus the Savior is alive! Let the children do some running now. Just for fun, let the children wear Bible costumes as they run several races. (Costumes are easily made from lengths of fabric cut with a center slot opening to place over the head. Tie the robes at the waist. Make sure the robes are not so long that someone trips and falls.)

Prepare for another activity by setting out overturned chairs under which you have placed colorful scarves, at least two per chair. Point out that butterflies are a picture symbol that can remind us of Jesus at Easter. Explain, **Butterflies begin as caterpillars.** Have the children crawl around on the floor like caterpillars. **Then the caterpillars go into a cocoon.** Have each child curl up under an over-turned chair (cocoon). **Then they break free of the cocoon, coming out as beautiful, glorious butterflies.** One at a time, tip over each child's chair and have them wave the scarves as if they are butterfly wings and they are flying around the room. After everyone has "flown" for a while, be seated and explain that the cocoon reminds us of Jesus' tomb. **The butterfly breaking out of the cocoon reminds us of Jesus breaking out of death and the grave with all His power and glory.**

REVIEWING
You can read this as a poem or sing it to the melody of "Christ the Lord Is Risen Today" (*Little Ones Sing Praise*, p. 96; note that this melody does not have alleluias). Consider having the children echo, repeating each line that you say or sing.

Jesus rose on Easter Day.
See! The stone was rolled away.
Angels showed the empty tomb.
Joy has chased away all gloom.

What a busy, happy day.
Ev'ryone had much to say,
"We saw Jesus with our eyes!
From the dead He did arise!"

Jesus is our God so true.
There is nothing He can't do.
Jesus took our sins away
So we'll live in heav'n someday!

LIVING
Bring out Lucas the Lamb, who says that Easter reminds him a lot of Christmas. Say, **Really! Why is that?** Lucas can then make comparisons: Both are very happy days when we sing happy songs. Angels gave important messages about Jesus on both days. At Christmas there was new life for baby Jesus, and at Easter there was new life for the risen Savior. We even use special flowers to decorate both days—poinsettias at Christmas and lilies at Easter. Shepherds ran to Bethlehem to see the Savior; friends of Jesus ran to Jerusalem to say they had seen the Savior. But the most important connection is that Christmas and Easter were all part of God's plan for our salvation!

SINGING
Sing "Glory, Glory, Lord Jesus" and "Jesus Lives! Alleluia, Amen!" (*Lift Little Voices*, pp. 27 and 29 and on CD). Both songs are somewhat lengthy, so you may want to cue the children in on just the refrains or repeated phrases.

CREATING
Make a butterfly from the flaps of two envelopes of the same size. Have children cut off the flaps. Place the middle points together (longer, flat ends to the sides). Lick the glue on one midpoint and overlap it onto the other to connect the two butterfly wings. Then decorate the wings with markers, glitter glue, sequins, and so on.

For another Easter project, in advance, one per child, draw the simple shape of a butterfly on white paper, using a marker to make a thick outline. Children are to cover the picture with waxed paper. Then they are to dip lengths of thick yarn into a bowl of white glue till the yarn is thoroughly covered. (Provide toothpicks for children who don't want to touch it, and also wet wipes for clean up.) Have them shape the yarn around the outlined drawing, making sure that all lines touch or cross each other. After the shape dries (at least overnight) it can be carefully peeled off the waxed paper and hung from thread on a window or as a wall hanging. To make it look like stained glass, glue on a piece of colored cellophane cut to shape.

CLOSING
Have an Easter Parade, not for Easter hats or Easter clothing, but to celebrate the true meaning of Easter—that our Savior, Jesus, has won the victory over sin, death, and the devil. Sing this song and other Easter songs as you march together around the room. (Use the tune of "The Farmer in the Dell.")

Jesus is alive! Jesus is alive!
Let's all sing and shout hooray
For Jesus is alive!

From an open Bible read today's words to remember from 1 Thessalonians 4:14: **We believe that Jesus died and rose again.**

26 Thomas Sees the Risen Savior
John 20:19–31

Theme: Believe in our risen Savior.

GATHERING
Have children sort objects by how they feel, using the sense of touch. Label four boxes with words and objects: 1—*SOFT,* with a swatch of fake fur attached; 2—*HARD,* with a rock attached; 3—*SMOOTH,* with a swatch of plastic or vinyl; 4—*ROUGH,* with sandpaper attached. Set out items such as cotton balls, wire mesh, cereal, and so on for the children to sort into the boxes. (Some items may fit more than one category.) Say, **We can learn a lot about things by touching them. In today's Bible story, a man named Thomas wanted to touch Jesus so he could know for certain that Jesus is alive.**

OPENING
Let children look through a pair of binoculars and a magnifying glass. Say, **Binoculars help us see something that is far away. A magnifying glass helps us see something that is very tiny. But there are some things we can't see—like the wind—but we know the wind is there. We can't see Jesus, but we know that He is here. In today's Bible story, Thomas wanted to see Jesus as well as touch Him. Then Thomas said he would believe that Jesus had risen from the dead. In the Bible, Jesus gives a blessing to all of us who have never seen Jesus or touched Him and yet we believe in Him. Listen to the words of Jesus, "Blessed are those who have not seen and yet have believed" (John 20:29). Let's learn more about this.**

LEARNING
Display last session's poster picture and review briefly the events of Easter morning. Then point out that the busy activity continued through the day. Toward evening two followers of Jesus were walking home from Jerusalem to the little town of Emmaus when Jesus Himself began to walk with them and explain all that had happened. Later the two disciples ran back to tell their friends in Jerusalem. (If you are using the book *Journey to Easter,* numbers 9 and 10 correspond with this lesson.) Meanwhile the disciples in Jerusalem were hiding in a room with locked doors. They were afraid of Jesus' enemies. (At this time show 10 clothespin puppets or draw 10 stick figures.) Show that one of the disciples, Thomas, is at a distance, not with the others. Then display a picture of Jesus with the disciples and read His words from John 20:19–22. Take Jesus away and add Thomas to the group of disciples. Read his reaction in John 20:24–25. Emphasize that Jesus did not get mad at Thomas, Jesus was not impatient or insulted, Jesus didn't walk away and say, "No second chance for you." Instead, Jesus came back, just for Thomas. **Jesus loves us so much. He comes looking for those who are lost in sin or who are weak in faith. We don't find Jesus—He finds us!** Return Jesus to the scene and read John 20:26–29. Distribute the children's page, compare it to the poster picture, and note that the scars on Jesus' hands are missing. Have children draw the imprints. Then ask if they have ever had "owies," scabs, or scars. They will want to talk about this. As they do this, place two small Band-Aids in the shape of a cross on the palm of each child's hand. Say, **This is a reminder that Jesus had scars from the nails that nailed Him to the cross. He suffered this to take away our sins. We thank Jesus for all that He did for us!**

MOVING
Do a little Easter celebrating, though in a secular way. Have the children go on an egg hunt, searching the room for plastic eggs you set out earlier. Set a limit on the number each child can find; once they find their quota, they may help someone else. Then have an egg-rolling contest after setting masking tape boundaries. (The symbolism of Easter eggs will be discussed later.)

REVIEWING
Have the children imitate your hand motions as you retell the Bible story: **Easter evening, 10 of Jesus' disciples were in a locked room.** *(Hold up 10 fingers.)* **They were afraid Jesus' enemies would hurt them too.** *(Wiggle hands, shaking with fear.)* **Suddenly Jesus was in the room with them. He said, "Peace be with you!"** *(Raise hands in blessing.)* **Jesus showed them the nail marks on His hands.** *(Hold open palms, side by side.)* **The disciples were overjoyed!** *(Clap your hands.)* **Later, when they told Thomas, who had not been with them, he said, "Oh, no! I don't believe it."** *(Shake index finger sideways to indicate NO.)* **Thomas said, "Unless I touch the marks on His hands, I will not believe."** *(Rub each palm with your fingers.)* **That next week, the same group of ten,** *plus Thomas,* **were gathered in the same room.** *(Hold up 10 fingers, and then switch to one.)* **Jesus appeared again and invited Thomas to see for himself.** *(Extend arms out as if welcoming.)* **Thomas immediately praised Jesus, saying, "My Lord and my God!"** *(Fold your hands.)* **Then Jesus gave a special blessing to you and me. He said, "Blessed are those who have not seen and yet have believed."** *(Motion toward the children.)*

LIVING
Bring out Lucas the Lamb, who is struggling to hold several plastic Easter eggs. He says, **Teacher, I don't get it. We had fun with Easter eggs today. But what do eggs have to do with Easter?** Explain that eggs remind us of something we can learn about Jesus. Just like a baby bird breaks out of a shell to new life, Jesus broke out of the grave at Easter to new life. The shell breaks when a baby chick hatches; the stone was rolled away when Jesus arose. Lucas says, **I get it now! We aren't celebrating eggs or birds or springtime, we are celebrating that Jesus is alive!**

SINGING
It is important to repeat new songs to help children remember them. So again sing the Easter songs "Glory, Glory, Lord Jesus" and "Jesus Lives! Alleluia, Amen!" (*Lift Little Voices,* pp. 27 and 29 and on CD). If the songs are too lengthy for your children, simply cue them in so they can join with the repeated refrains.

CREATING
Reinforce the concept of the Easter egg symbolism. Using fun foam (or colored paper) and egg-shaped patterns, have the children trace, decorate, and cut out Easter egg shapes. Then have the children cut a jagged line across the center of the egg to "crack" it in half. Next, have the children make yellow fun foam baby chicks (a circle body with a smaller circle for the head, dots for eyes, and an inverted triangle for a beak). It would be best to again work from patterns to get the appropriate size. Glue the baby chick to the back of one egg half (most of the chick should still be visible). Then reattach the two egg halves on the left side with a metal brad (with adult assistance). Now the children will be able to close and then open the egg to show the chick—the new life—that is breaking out of the egg shell.

Point out that we see a lot of flowers at Easter, but that is not just because of springtime. Again, flowers can be a reminder of Jesus. A seed seems lifeless until a flower breaks out of it and grows. Jesus was lifeless in the grave, but by the power of God Jesus broke out of death and the grave in all His glory. Let each of the children make three Easter flowers. These can be made from colored paper or fun foam. Children are to cut out four heart shapes (of various colors) and attach them near the top of a wooden craft stick (demonstrate a north, south, east, west position with points meeting at the center). At the center of the flower attach a yellow circle. For the vase, turn a Styrofoam cup upside down and poke the stem ends of the craft stick flowers through the cup base to hold the flowers in place. Decorate the vases with stickers.

CLOSING
Thomas's words of faith are today's Bible words to remember from John 20:28: **My Lord and my God.** As you say the Lord's Prayer, have the children respond with Thomas's words at each asterisk. Pray together in that faith in the Lord. **Our Father who art in heaven, hallowed be Thy name. * Thy kingdom come, Thy will be done on earth as it is in heaven. * Give us this day our daily bread; and forgive us our trespasses as we forgive those who trespass against us. * And lead us not into temptation, but deliver us from evil. * For Thine is the kingdom and the power and the glory forever and ever. Amen.**

27 Philip and the Man from Africa

Acts 8:26–40

Theme: Jesus washes away our sins.

GATHERING
Let the children explore at a sand table or plastic tub partly filled with sand. Provide cups, sieves, and scoops. Add Bible-times clothespin puppets and plastic horses. Say, **Today we will hear a Bible story that takes place in a dry, sandy, rocky desert. One man was walking, and the other rode in a chariot pulled by horses.**

OPENING
Say, **In the Bible story, the man in the chariot was reading a book.** Hold up a scroll you have made by rolling a length of paper at both ends, with the italicized words below printed on it. Hold the end rolls of paper in your right and left hand. **This is a strange looking book! But this is the kind of book people used in Bible times. They did not have machines to make the kinds of books we have today with covers and pages and pictures. Instead, people wrote out all the words on long strips of paper. The man in our story was reading the Book of Isaiah in the Bible. The words of the prophet Isaiah said,** *"He was led like a sheep to the slaughter . . . His life was taken."* **The man didn't understand. He wondered what the words meant. Let's learn more about what happened.**

LEARNING
Explain, **This man was on his way home to Africa. God wanted this man to know the truth about God's Word. So an angel of the Lord sent Philip, a follower of Jesus, to that desert road. The man from Africa invited Philip to join him in his chariot to explain what the Bible words meant. Philip said the words were talking about God's promise to send a Savior to take away our sins. Then Philip told the man the Good News that God had already kept His promise. Philip said:**

"The prophet says our Savior dear
Will suffer pain and strife.
He'll die to take away our sins
And give eternal life.
This promise God has truly kept
Through Jesus, His own Son.
Christ died, then rose on Easter morn.
The vict'ry has been won!"

Explain that the man from Africa now not only understood, he also believed and wanted to be baptized. (Note: The previous and the following poem verses are taken from the book *The Gospel Good News Goes to Africa.* This is available from Concordia Publishing House and not only has additional poem verses and a glossary, it also has wonderful pictures to help children better understand this important story.)

At last, the Bible's words were clear.
The happy man now smiled,
"Because of Jesus, I'm forgiven.
His grace makes me God's child!
Look! There's some water over there!
Please baptize me this minute
Into the name of God the Son,
The Father, and the Spirit!"

MOVING
Have the children walk on the lines on the floor of the gym (or lines you have drawn with chalk on the playground or placed with masking tape in your room). Say, **Let's pretend that we are traveling in a chariot going to Africa. The lines on the floor show the road and the way home.** Also play a racing game in which children are paired up. One child is the "chariot," and the other child is the driver standing behind the "chariot" and holding onto the reins (shoulders) of the chariot.

REVIEWING
Distribute the children's pages. Compare them to the poster picture and discover what is missing. (The pond of water.) Say, **Philip and the man from Africa were very lucky to find water out in the middle of the dry desert. Actually, that is not true! It was not a matter of luck. It was part of God's plan. It was another example of God pouring out His blessings.** Point out that the man had already heard God's Word and believed in Jesus. But the waters of Baptism, connected to God's Word, gave Him yet another gift from God. **Everyone likes gifts! And this man too was eager to receive God's gift of Baptism. How does the water in Baptism wash away our sins? This happens through God's Word. Remember, the Word of God is very powerful. God said the words, and the world was created. So of course, when God said the words that Baptism brings us faith and forgiveness in Jesus, we know God's Word is powerful and will do it! In Mark 16:16, God's Word says, "Whoever believes and is baptized will be saved."**

LIVING
Bring out Lucas the Lamb, who says, **My favorite thing about this Bible story is that God cared about this one person. Sometimes God's Word is preached to hundreds and thousands of people! But God also cares about each and every one of you. Jesus told a story about that. Jesus said that a shepherd had 100 sheep. He brought them home one evening and counted each one as they entered the sheep pen. The shepherd counted 99. One of the sheep was missing. He didn't say, "Oh, well, I've got lots of other sheep." No, the shepherd left the 99 sheep and went looking for the one lamb that was missing. He celebrated joyfully when he found the little lamb. Jesus is the Good Shepherd. He cares about every one of you. You are important to Him. Jesus takes care of you and rescues you from sin. Jesus cared about that one man in the desert. Jesus cares about you!**

SINGING
Sing the songs on pages 97 and 98 of *Little Ones Sing Praise:* "I Was Baptized," "Baptism Song," and "Child of God." Assure your children who are not baptized that they are saved by the power of the Holy Spirit working through God's Word, and they can look forward to the day when they receive the special gift of Baptism.

CREATING
Make sparkling water-drop baptismal mobiles. Have children sprinkle glitter onto the sticky side of a sheet of clear contact paper. Cover this with a second sheet of clear contact paper. Provide poster paper patterns of water drops (ovals that come to a point at the top). Children may trace and cut out three of these shapes on the glitter paper they have prepared. Paper punch a hole at the top of each water drop. Tie string through each hole and tape the other end of the string to the bottom of a plastic clothes hanger. Hang the mobiles in your room and explain that the three water drops stand for baptizing in the name of the Father and of the Son and of the Holy Spirit, just as Jesus commanded.

Consider that Philip and the man from Africa were very different from each other: they came from different countries, it is likely they had different skin colors, and the African man was probably rich while Philip was poor. But these things don't matter to God, and they should not matter to us. **The Bible tells us that God wants all people to be saved. He cares about each one of us.** Give each child a blue paper plate to stand for the earth. Provide multicultural paper (in varying shades of beige to dark brown, available at teacher stores) or multicultural crayons to make people shapes of various skin colors. Provide simple gingerbread boy cookie cutters that children can trace around to make the people. The people can be left on a square background or they can be cut out, depending on the ability of the children. The people shapes may then be attached with tape either to the rim of the paper plates or at a north, south, east, west position at the center of the paper plates. **God loves all the people of the world and wants them to hear the truth of God's Word.**

CLOSING
Sing "Jesus Loves the Little Children" (*Little Ones Sing Praise,* p. 94) and "You've Got to Tell" (*Lift Little Voices,* p. 42 and on CD). From the Bible read Jesus' words in Matthew 28:18–20. Also read today's Bible words to remember from Acts 22:16: **Get up, be baptized and wash your sins away.**

28 Rhoda and Friends Pray for Peter — Acts 12:1–18

Theme: Worship and pray together.

GATHERING

Set out a variety of locks and keys for the children to explore. As they work, say, **Locks and locked doors are an important part of today's Bible story. We will see that no lock is stronger than the power of God. As the Bible says in Luke 1:37: "Nothing is impossible with God."**

OPENING

Tell the children a few "Knock, Knock" jokes. Even if they don't understand the punch line, they will enjoy the repetition. Add jokes of your own choosing.

Knock, knock. *Who's there?*
Ima. *Ima who?*
(sing) **Ima little teapot, short and stout.**

Knock, knock. *Who's there?*
Orange. *Orange who?*
Orange you glad you came here today!

Continue by explaining that in today's Bible story the disciple Peter really did knock on a door (make a knocking sound). When a girl named Rhoda finally opened the door to see who was there, she got a big surprise, and so did he!

LEARNING

Focus on seven key words that describe the people in the Bible story. Use facial expressions as you identify each word.

1. Evil. The story begins with a very bad, evil man—King Herod. The king had Peter arrested and thrown in jail. The only thing Peter had done was to tell people that Jesus is the Savior, who died and arose at Easter to save us from sin.

2. Trusting. Peter knew that the king could put him to death. But Peter wasn't afraid. Even though Peter was tied up with two chains and surrounded by guards, he trusted that God was with him. He didn't worry; he quietly fell asleep.

3. Amazed. Peter was amazed at God's rescue plan: an angel woke him up; his chains fell off; no guards moved to stop him; and the iron door of the jail opened up.

4. Excited. At first Peter thought he was dreaming, but then he realized that he really was free. He hurried to the home of his friends to tell them how God had rescued him. Many of Peter's friends were gathered at that house, praying for him!

5. Surprised. Peter knocked at the door of the home. Rhoda was so surprised to hear Peter's voice, she didn't even open the door for him! She ran back to tell the others.

6. Distrust. The friends distrusted Rhoda's good news. They said, "You're out of your mind." They thought she was crazy. But then they could hear Peter, still knocking.

7. Joyful. When they opened the door, they rejoiced. God had answered their prayers. Peter was safe. **As the Bible says, "Nothing is impossible with God."** Distribute the children's pages and have them add the look of surprise to Rhoda's face.

MOVING

Play a Hot Potato game. Children are to sit on chairs in a circle and pass a small ball (hot potato) quickly from child to child as music plays. When the music stops, the child holding the "hot potato" sits on the floor. Let all children continue playing. If a child seated on the floor ends up with the hot potato, that child may select the next person to be seated on the floor. The game ends when all children are seated on the floor. After this game, get the children moving, having them all be hot potatoes. They can wiggle and jump freely as music plays. They all sit down when the music stops.

REVIEWING

Use two shoe boxes and several clothespin puppets to review the Bible story. Remove the lid from both boxes and cut a door in the long side of each. Stand clothespin puppets (or stick puppets) in play-dough bases to make them stand. Retell the story, using the first box to represent the prison in Jerusalem. Put guards inside the box, with Peter sleeping between them. Add an angel who leads Peter through the door that amazingly opened. Then move Peter to the other box, which has a closed door and clothespin puppets inside (people gathered for prayer). Show Peter knocking, Rhoda coming to the door, and surprisingly, the door stays closed! Continue with the story and the people finally opening the door to welcome Peter in. Say, **God rescued Peter in an amazing way. God rescued each of us in an even more amazing way when He sent His own Son, Jesus, to die on the cross to take away our sins and to arise at Easter to offer us eternal life with Him in heaven! Amazing!**

LIVING

Bring out Lucas the Lamb, who holds a ziplock plastic bag filled with green grass. Lucas says, **In the Bible story, Peter's friends gathered together to pray. Let's make a special book of prayers. I am thankful for the green pastures where I have plenty of grass to eat. What are you thankful for?** Give each child a ziplock bag and allow time for them to find something for which they are thankful. Set out catalogues and magazines if they wish to find a picture rather than an object. Then gather the bags, staple them together on the side, and look at one "page" at a time as you say a prayer that includes the many things for which the children give thanks.

SINGING

Sing the "Thank You Song" (*Lift Little Voices*, p. 34 and on the CD). Then pray the following words or sing them to the melody on page 15 of *Little Ones Sing Praise*.

1. We pray for each other, For sister and brother,
   For father and mother; Dear God, bless us all.
2. We pray for the sick ones, The strong and the weak ones,
   The brave and the meek ones; Dear God, bless us all.
3. We ask this through Jesus, Our Savior, who loves us
   And from our sin frees us. Dear God, bless us all.

CREATING

Emphasize that God is with us everywhere. God was even with Peter in jail. God doesn't promise to always stop our troubles, but He will be with us to help us through our problems. Jesus said, "I am with you always" (Matthew 28:20). Have the children make reminders of one of the many places where God is with us—He is with us as we travel in our family cars. Have the children make "sun visor art," using 6×9-inch envelopes (available at office supply stores). Children may print a message that has a cross, heart, and the letter U (which means "Jesus loves you"). Be sure that the message is printed the correct way (lengthwise) so that the envelope can slide over the visor. Children may add other decorations to the visor art. Note: The envelope should be placed on the passenger side to avoid obstructing the driver's view.

Make a picture of the greatest rescue: on the cross, Jesus rescued us from sin, death, and the power of the devil. Give each child a cross shape cut from a 9×12-inch piece of poster paper. Cut small slits around the outside edges of the cross, each about an inch apart. Provide a colorful assortment of yarn, each piece a yard in length. Assist the children as they wrap the yarn around the cross, securing the yarn through the slits. Children may switch colors. They may also cross the yarn at various angles (not just straight across). They can, but do not have to cover the cross with yarn. They can determine when they are finished. Loose edges may need to be taped on the back. Punch a hole at the top of the cross and attach a yarn loop hanger.

CLOSING

Discuss: How could Peter sleep when he was in such great danger? (His friend James had been killed by this same King Herod just days earlier.) The answer is that Peter trusted the faithfulness of God. He knew God would do what was best. Peter was surrounded by God's care and rescued by God's angel. The Bible says in Psalm 32:10: **The Lord's unfailing love surrounds the man who trusts in Him.** And in Psalm 125:2 it says: **As the mountains surround Jerusalem, so the Lord surrounds His people both now and forevermore.** Pray, pointing to indicate the italicized positions: **Dear Lord, be with us each day. Surround us with Your holy angels *before* us, *behind* us, and *beside* us. In Jesus' holy name we pray. Amen.** Close by reading today's Bible words to remember from Psalm 91:11: **[God] will command His angels . . . to guard you in all your ways.**

29 God Makes Saul a "New Creation" *Acts 9:1–22*

Theme: God brings us to faith in Jesus.

GATHERING
In an open area or outdoors, let the children make soap bubbles, using plastic wands. Ask, **How is the soapy liquid changed into a floating bubble?** (It is filled with air as we blow into or wave the plastic wand.) **In today's Bible story, we will hear about a man who was changed from a bad man to a believer in Jesus. How was he changed? God filled his heart with faith. God changed his heart and his life. God gives us faith too and changes us to be His very own people!**

OPENING
Demonstrate another change, emphasizing the term "a new creation." Display a large Styrofoam meat tray. Let the children watch as you cut out a large cross shape from the tray. Then decorate it using permanent marking pens. Place it on a cookie sheet and bake it at 250 degrees for 2–3 minutes. When you take it out of the oven, say, **We have a new creation. We no longer have a large meat tray. It has changed into a small, but pretty cross.** The cross will have shrunk to about ¼ of its original size. (Caution: Do not let the children touch the oven or the hot materials.) **Today we will hear how God changed a man named Saul into a new creation. Saul didn't look different after Jesus changed him, but his actions and words changed.**

LEARNING
Have the children imitate your actions as you tell the Bible story. **Saul did not like people who were followers of Jesus.** *(Make an angry face.)* **One day Saul and his helpers were walking on a road.** *(Walk in place.)* **They were going to the town of Damascus where they wanted to capture the Christians and throw them in jail.** *(Pretend to grab a person.)* **Suddenly a bright light from heaven flashed around Saul.** *(Cover your eyes in fear.)* **Saul fell to the ground when he heard the voice of God speaking to him.** *(Drop to the ground, still covering your eyes.)* **God said, "Saul, why are you hurting Me?" Saul asked, "Who are you?" The voice said, "I am Jesus. You are hurting My people. Now go to the city and you will be told what to do." When Saul got up, he was blind. He couldn't see anything.** *(Stand up, walk around with closed eyes, arms stretched out in front of you.)* **His helpers had to lead him into the town of Damascus. Saul just sat there.** *(Sit in a chair.)* **He couldn't see anything and he didn't eat or drink anything. He just waited, for three days.** *(Hold up three fingers.)* **After three days, God sent Ananias, a believer in Jesus, to the house on Straight Street where Saul was staying. Ananias put his hands on Saul and something like scales fell from his eyes and he could see again.** *(Rub your eyes, open them joyfully.)* **Ananias baptized Saul in the name of the Father, Son, and Holy Spirit.** *(Pretend to pour water three times by hand.)* **Saul was now a Christian! He believed in Jesus! He spent the rest of his life telling people the Good News about what our Savior did for us!** *(Make the sign of the cross.)* On the children's pages, color in the rays of light that the Bible speaks of in Acts 9:3. (This also reminds us of the voice of Jesus coming down from heaven.)

MOVING
Play a game somewhat like Pin the Tail on the Donkey. However, this will be Take Saul to Damascus. Post a large sheet of paper on which you have drawn a Bible-times city (lots of square adobe houses). When it is a child's turn, the child is to take a picture of a Bible-times man with a tape roll on his back and stick him onto the picture of the city. However, first you must blindfold the child, recalling that Saul was unable to see. Another variation: Saul had helpers to lead him, so whenever the child strays from a path to the picture, two chosen helpers may assist. Also consider playing "life-size tic-tac-toe." Mark a giant tic-tac-toe grid on the ground with chalk or masking tape. Divide into teams of *O*s and *X*s, each team member holding up a paper with a large *O* or *X* on it. One at a time, children stand in a tic-tac-toe section until one of the teams gets three in a row.

REVIEWING
In advance, prepare a puppet face made from a paper or plastic plate that is divided into three sections. With the largest section at the bottom, draw a smile on the face with a red marker. In each of the two smaller sections at the top, draw a solid circle for the eyes. Tape tan circles to the sides of the face for ears. Tape an arching section of dark brown paper at the top for hair. Attach a ruler at the bottom for a handle. Also have available two white paper circles on which you have drawn closed eyelids (like small smile shapes). Introduce the puppet as the man named Saul. Read his story from the Bible. When you read that he was blind, use tape rolls to place the white circles over the puppet's eyes. When you read that scales fell from his eyes and he could see again, peel off the white circles and drop them to the ground. After concluding the story, hold up the puppet again and say, **This is Saul before he met Jesus.** Set the puppet down and then hold it up again and say, **This is Saul after he met Jesus. Saul was a new person. But he didn't look any different. What was new about Saul?** (His heart, his actions, his life; he believed in Jesus, he lived for Jesus, he became a baptized Christian.) Read 2 Corinthians 5:17: **"Therefore, if anyone is in Christ, he is a new creation; the old has gone, the new has come!" Jesus gets rid of the old sinful self in each of us as He forgives our sins; He leads us to be new people who live for Him!**

LIVING
Bring out Lucas the Lamb, who says, **I think I've heard this Bible story before. But I thought the man's name was Paul.** Explain that Saul and Paul are the same person. Sometimes people have more than one name. Lucas says, **Oh, I get it. It's like my name is Lucas, but my dad calls me Luke and my big sister calls me Fuzzy.** Point out that from now on we usually call Saul "Paul." This can help us remember that Saul-Paul was a changed person, a new creation. Next lesson we will have another story about Saul-Paul, because he became a missionary who traveled all over the world, telling people that Jesus is our Savior!

SINGING
Say, **God chose Saul-Paul to tell many people about Jesus. God also chooses us to tell others. We can talk to our friends and family. We can remind them that God loves them, forgives them, and takes care of them.** Sing about this in "God So Loved the World" and "You've Got to Tell" (*Lift Little Voices*, pp. 33 and 42 and on CD).

CREATING
Jesus cleans our hearts by forgiving our sins. He fills our hearts with faith and makes us new people, a new creation, children of God. Make cross and heart symbols as reminders of this. Here are several project possibilities. Have children use a permanent marking pen to trace two heart and two cross shapes on clear plastic acetate sheets (available from craft and office supply stores). Cut out the shapes; place similar shapes back to back; staple the edges together except for a two-inch opening; stuff each shape with a variety of colors of tissue paper that has been cut into ½-inch wide strips; staple the opening shut; staple a yarn loop at the top; use as a wall or window hanging. Or make toothpaste pictures on colored paper. (Different colors of toothpaste will add interest too.) Have children use a pencil to trace around a cross and a heart shape. Retrace the lines with lines of toothpaste, squeezing lightly for a thin line effect, or squeezing harder for a thicker line. Set aside the pictures to dry. Or, with appropriate permission, have children make heart and cross shapes using chalk on sidewalks and parking lots. Suggest that shapes can be combined—a cross with a heart at the center or a heart with a cross at the center.

CLOSING
Point out that God chose Saul-Paul to be a follower of Jesus. God also chooses us. As Jesus said in John 15:16: **You did not choose Me, but I chose you.** Thank God in prayer for the blessings of forgiveness and faith. Ask Him to help you live each day as His new creation, a baptized child of God. From an open Bible read today's words to remember from 2 Corinthians 5:17: **If anyone is in Christ, he is a new creation; the old has gone, the new has come!**

30 Paul and Silas Sing for Joy in Jail
Acts 16:22–34

Theme: God is with us at all times.

GATHERING
Provide each child with colorful scarves and streamers to wave as you sing songs of praise to God. **Today we will hear another story about Saul, only now we will use his other name—Paul. He and his friend Silas sang songs of praise to God. They couldn't move around like you just did. But they still could use their voices.**

OPENING
Display two chains. The first chain should be a beautiful chain necklace. Say, **This chain makes me think of happy times. I wear this chain when I get dressed up to go to a party or to a nice restaurant.** Then show a very heavy, industrial chain; if possible, let the children hold it. **This chain does not make me think of happy times. In our Bible story, Paul and Silas were in jail. Their hands and feet were locked in chains so they couldn't move. But even at a bad time like that, Paul and Silas were happy because they knew God was still with them and loved them. Even wearing chains in jail, Paul and Silas sang songs of thanks to God. The Bible tells us in 1 Thessalonians 5:18, "Give thanks in all circumstances." That means, whatever happens, good or bad, we can thank and praise God for His love and salvation in Christ Jesus. Nothing can change that.**

LEARNING
In advance prepare (or have the children prepare) individual paper chains, using tape to attach loops of gray paper. Have the children sit on the floor in a circle with hands folded. Place a paper chain over the wrists of each child. Explain that Paul and Silas had been treated unfairly. Enemies beat them and threw them into jail. The only thing they had done was talk about Jesus the Savior. **It was late at night. The jail was dark and damp. Paul and Silas were singing and praying to God. The other prisoners in the jail were listening to them.** Explain that suddenly there was an earthquake. Shake all over and toss off your paper chain, inviting the children to do the same. Explain that the jail guard was afraid he would be punished for letting the prisoners escape, but Paul calmed him by saying that everyone was still there. The jailer must have been listening to the hymns and prayers too, because he asked how he could be saved. He wanted to become a new creation too. **The Bible gives us Paul's answer in Acts 16:31: "Believe in the Lord Jesus, and you will be saved."** Have the children stand up and walk with you to another part of the room as you explain that the jailer took Paul and Silas into his own home to tell his whole family about Jesus. **The jailer and his whole family were baptized in the name of the Father and of the Son and of the Holy Spirit.** The jailer used water to wash and clean Paul and Silas's wounds; Paul used water and God's Word to baptize the family, as their sins were washed away through the cleansing power of Jesus.

MOVING
Try a rhythmic chant in which you name a part of the body and tap it, to an 8-count beat. Children can imitate your tapping and counting. For example, tap on your knees as you say: **Knees-2-3-4-5-6-7-8.** Tap your toes as you say: **Toes-2-3-4-5-6-7-8.** Continue in this manner. For more active movement, play Protect the Pin. Have the children form a circle. At the center of the circle place a bowling pin. Children are to use a rubber ball to try to knock the pin over. One volunteer stands guard at the center of the circle and tries to protect the pin. When the pin falls (even if the guard knocks it over accidentally), a new guard is chosen.

REVIEWING
Point out that many amazing things happened in this Bible story. **We could call these events *amazing, astonishing, fantastic, extraordinary,* or *outstanding*. But today we will use the word *remarkable!*** As you review the story, have the children join you in repeating the phrase *That's remarkable!* Cue them in by lifting up your Bible. **1) The other prisoners had never seen anything like it. Paul and Silas were in a terrible place—in jail. But they were joyfully singing praise and thanks to God.** *That's remarkable!* **2) Earthquakes can be dangerous. But God sent an earthquake that set them free! Everyone's chains fell off and the prison doors flew open.** *That's remarkable!* **3) All the prisoners could have escaped. But they all stayed right there.** *That's remarkable!* **4) Amazingly, the jailer listened to his prisoners Paul and Silas. He wanted what they already had—a Savior!** *That's remarkable!* **5) Next, instead of locking up the prisoners, the jailer took his prisoners—Paul and Silas—into his own home. He could have gotten into trouble for that. But it was more important to him to know about Jesus and be baptized.** *That's remarkable!* **6) The most outstanding part of the whole story is that Jesus is *our* Savior too. Jesus died on the cross and arose at Easter to take away the sins of Paul, Silas, the jailer, you and me, and all believers.** *That's remarkable!*

LIVING
Bring out Lucas the Lamb, who reads a poem that his friend wrote to remind the children that God is always with us, so we can be happy and joyful whatever happens, in all circumstances, good or bad, because we know we are saved now and eternally.

1. The Lord God is with you wherever you are,
   Whether it's nearby or whether it's far,
   Alone in your room or with Mom in a car,
   The Lord God is with you wherever you are.

2. The Lord God is with you each day and each night,
   With either the sun or the stars shining bright.
   You know He is there with His power and His might.
   The Lord God is with you each day and each night.

3. I'll praise God forever and songs I will sing,
   For Christ is my Savior and most holy King.
   He promises heaven—to that I will cling.
   I'll praise God forever and songs I will sing.

SINGING
Since the children will be singing praise songs at the beginning and end of the session, sing songs now just for fun. Sing "The Loud and Soft Song" and "God's Little Beetle" (*Lift Little Voices,* pp. 65 and 76 and on the CD).

CREATING
Say, **Paul and Silas sang hymns and prayed to God while they were in prison. The jailer heard the Word of God about Jesus his Savior right there in that jail. Let's make a picture of the special place we go to where we sing, pray, and hear God's Word together.** Make pictures of a church. Give each child a large triangle of poster paper. Draw vertical lines near the left and right side points and fold back to make a base so that the church building can stand. Tape a yellow paper cross to the top point. Demonstrate how the children can draw a door and two windows on the church. Then turn it over and fill the church with people by cutting pictures of people from magazines and catalogues and gluing them in place, either at random or standing in rows.

In another project, make a picture of Paul's message: "To preach Christ crucified" (1 Corinthians 1:23). Instead of painting a cross with water, try painting with ice! In advance make ice cube "paintbrushes" by inserting wooden craft sticks into partially frozen ice cubes. Then freeze the ice cubes solid. Sprinkle dry tempera paint powder onto each child's sheet of paper. Let each child hold an ice cube paintbrush by the handle and rub it back and forth, swirling it over the powdered paint in the shape of a cross. As the ice cube melts, the water will mix with the paint. Let the paintings dry and then shake off the excess powder into a container.

CLOSING
Like Paul and Silas, sing songs of thanks and praise to God. From an open Bible read today's words to remember spoken by Paul to the guard at the jail, and also to you and me in Acts 16:31: **Believe in the Lord Jesus, and you will be saved.** Stand in a circle, holding hands as you close with this blessing:

**Go as God's children, blessed from above,
Forgiven to live a new life of love.**

Appendix: Snacks

CAUTION: BE AWARE OF CHILDREN'S FOOD ALLERGIES, ESPECIALLY TO PEANUTS. ADAPT ACCORDINGLY.

1. Cinnamon Crisps: Mix 6 tablespoons sugar and ½ teaspoon cinnamon. Brush the top of 6 flour tortillas lightly with corn syrup and sprinkle with the cinnamon mixture. Cut each tortilla into wedges and place on a baking sheet. Bake at 400 degrees for 10 minutes until golden and crisp. Serve alone or with applesauce as a dip.

2. Fruit Roll Ups: Unfold one refrigerated pie crust on a floured surface. Spread fruit jam over the crust. Cut into 20 wedges. Roll up, starting at the wide edge, pinching the point of the dough to seal in place. Refrigerate one hour. Line a cookie sheet with aluminum foil and grease with spray shortening and place roll ups 2 inches apart. Bake at 450 degrees for 10–12 minutes, until lightly browned. Optional: Drizzle thin icing on top.

3. Animal Trail Mix: Mix together 2 cups animal-shaped graham crackers, 1 cup salted peanuts, ½ cup M&Ms, and ½ cup raisins. Put mix in sandwich bags.

4. Fishies in the River: Wash and cut stalks of celery into 3-inch lengths. Fill with cream cheese or another type of cheese spread (tint with blue food coloring, if desired). Place fish-shaped crackers on the filling.

5. Fruit and Dip: Combine a small tub of low-fat cream cheese with ⅓ cup of undiluted frozen apple or orange juice concentrate and a pinch of cinnamon. Blend until smooth. Serve with apple and pear slices, strawberries, and banana chunks for dippers.

6. Gobblers: Unwrap candy caramels, soften each in your hands, and roll into a ball (turkey's body). Cut round fudge-striped shortbread cookies. Press one cookie half (turkey's feathers) into each caramel ball. Place this on a chocolate kiss (turkey feet), pressing slightly so it sticks to the caramel. Then press a piece of candy corn into the caramel to make the turkey's face.

7. Ring around the Rosey: Mix one jar (7 oz.) marshmallow crème with 1 (8 oz.) container of strawberry-flavored cream cheese. Beat until well blended. Refrigerate 1 hour. Place creamy mixture in a mound in the center of a large round serving plate. Alternate vanilla wafers with apple slices around the dip to resemble flower petals.

8. Cookie Pops: Insert wooden craft sticks into Newton-type fruit chewy cookies. Let children decorate cookies with decorating gels, frostings, and candy sprinkles.

9. Muffin Pan Snacks: Fix orange, lemon, or lime gelatin according to package directions. Divide mixture evenly among 6 cups of a muffin pan. Refrigerate about 45 minutes until thickened but not set. Finely chop fresh carrots or celery to make 1½ cups. Stir equal amounts into each of the cups of gelatin. Refrigerate about 2 hours until firm. When ready to unmold, dip bottom only of the muffin pan into warm water for 5–10 seconds. Run a knife around edge of each cup and gently lift gelatin from cups.

10. Carrot Pinwheels: Beat together 2 tablespoons softened cream cheese with 2 tablespoons ranch dressing. Spread evenly on 2 (8-inch) flour tortillas. Sprinkle with 1 cup finely shredded carrots. Roll tortillas up tightly and wrap in plastic wrap. Place in refrigerator for at least 30 minutes. When ready to serve, cut each roll into 6 pieces.

11. Walking Salad: Core small apples, one per child, but leave the bottoms on. Let children fill the core of the apples with small amounts of peanut butter, chocolate chips, and mini-marshmallows. Now they are ready to eat their salad while taking a walk.

12. Count to Six Salad: Prepare six bowls of fresh fruit cut into bite-size pieces (oranges, strawberries, bananas, seedless grapes) and other fruit salad ingredients (yogurt and orange juice concentrate). Give each child a bowl, instructing them to put one teaspoonful of each ingredient into their bowl while counting from 1–6. Have them stir their fruit salad six times. On the count of six they are ready to eat it!

13. Crunchy Banana Lollipops: Cut four bananas in half across the middle. Poke craft sticks into ends. Heat ½ cup peanut butter and ½ cup chocolate syrup together in a saucepan until smooth. Dip banana pops into the warm mixture and then roll in a bowl of fruit-flavored crispy rice cereal. Place on waxed paper and freeze 30 minutes.

14. Cantaloupe-Peach Smoothies: In a blender or a smoothie maker, mix 1 cup cantaloupe chunks, 1 cup sliced peaches, ½ cup vanilla yogurt, 1–2 tablespoons fresh lemon juice, and 2–3 tablespoons maple syrup. Pour into small cups and eat with a spoon.

15. Orange Frosties: Combine 2 cups milk, 1 cup water, 1 cup ice cubes, 3 tbsp. sugar, and one 6-ounce can of frozen orange juice concentrate in a blender and process until all the ice cubes are chopped and drink is frothy.

16. Popcorn Cake: Measure enough popped corn (removing uncooked kernels) to fill a Bundt cake pan. Pour popcorn onto a large piece of waxed paper. In a saucepan over low heat, melt 1 stick of butter. Add 40 large marshmallows one at a time, stirring constantly until all are melted. Pour the mixture over the popcorn carefully until it is covered. Sprinkle 1 pound M&Ms on top and mix it all together with hands that have been sprayed with nonstick cooking spray. Spray the cake pan, add the mixture, and let cool until firm. Remove from pan and cut into pieces with a large knife.

17. Frozen Grape Bonbons: Pick seedless red or green grapes off their stems, wash, and place on cookie sheets to freeze. When frozen, put in plastic bags for up to three months.

18. Dipsy Strawberries: Wash and pat dry a pint of strawberries, leaving on the hulls. Beat together one block (8 oz.) cream cheese with 3 tablespoons milk. Let children dip the berries in the cream mixture and then in a little bit of brown sugar.

19. S'Mores Snack: Make a mixture of 2 cups honey graham cereal, 1 cup miniature marshmallows, ½ cup mini or regular chocolate chips, ½ cup raisins, and 1 cup peanuts.

20. Pretzel Yummies: Combine a 14-ounce package of caramels and 1 tablespoon water. Stir over low heat until caramels are melted. Dip the top half of pretzel twists or pretzel rods in the caramel mixture to coat, letting the excess drip off. (If mixture is too runny, let it cool a bit.) Place pretzels on a buttered baking sheet to cool. Place 4 ounces semisweet chocolate and 1 teaspoon shortening in a pan over low heat and stir until melted. Spoon it into a small plastic bag with a small hole snipped out of one corner. Drizzle over pretzels and add decorative sprinkles. Cool in refrigerator for one hour.

21. Purple Cow: Combine 1 pint (2 cups) vanilla ice cream, 1 (6 oz.) can frozen grape juice concentrate, and 1½ cups milk in a blender and mix until smooth.

22. No-Bake Granola Bars: Combine ½ cup brown sugar and ½ cup light corn syrup in a saucepan and bring to a boil, stirring constantly. Remove from heat and stir in 1 cup peanut butter and 1 teaspoon vanilla. Add 1½ cups quick oats and 1½ cups crispy rice cereal, 1 cup raisins, ½ cup sunflower seeds, and 2 tablespoons sesame seeds. Press the mixture into a 9-inch square baking pan. Cool and cut into bars.

23. Creamy Fruit Dippers: Soften an 8-ounce package of cream cheese. Mix in 2 tablespoons orange juice and 1 jar marshmallow crème until smooth. Serve with apple or pear wedges, chunks of banana, pineapple, strawberries, or other fresh fruits.

24. Tropical Pops: Blend 2 cups pineapple juice and two bananas in a blender until smooth. Pour mixture into small paper cups and cover with foil. Make a slit in the center of each foil cover and insert a popsicle stick. Freeze.

25. Apple Pizzas: Using refrigerated breadstick dough, pat each stick into a flat, circular shape and place on a baking sheet. Slice ¼ of a peeled and chopped apple on top of each round. Using a mixture of ½ cup sugar and 3–4 teaspoons cinnamon, sprinkle tops of "pizzas." Place a thin slice of butter on top of each. Bake 350 degrees for 10–12 minutes.

26. PBJ Popovers: Place refrigerated biscuits on a cookie sheet. Pat out into 3-inch circles. Put a teaspoon of peanut butter and a teaspoon of jelly on each biscuit. Fold over each biscuit and pinch ends together to seal. Bake at 425 degrees for 10 to 12 minutes.

27. Applesauce on a Stick: In a blender or food processor, mix ½ cup unsweetened pineapple juice, 3 cups peeled apple slices, ¼ teaspoon cinnamon, ½ cup raisins. Add 1 or more tablespoons of sugar, to taste. Spoon mixture into paper cups, placing foil over each. Slit the foil and insert a wooden stick into each mixture. Freeze until solid.

28. Frozen Yogurtwiches: Spread graham cracker squares with fruit-flavored yogurt. Place another cracker square on top and freeze until serving time.

29. Happy Faces: Spread slices of bread with peanut butter. Make happy faces, placing two banana circles for eyes, one raisin for the nose, and M&Ms candies to form the smile.

30. Cheesy Muffin Melts: Cut English muffins in half. Put muffin halves on a foil-lined baking sheet. Top each muffin with a slice of cheese. Bake at 375 degrees until cheese is lightly browned and bubbly—about 20 minutes.